Calligraphy for Book Beginners

# Suggested Writing Tools:

- Calligraphy Pencils

- Mechanical Stationary Pencils

- Sketching pencils and sharpeners

- Fine tip of a Dual Tip Calligraphy Pen

- Fine tip of most brush pens

- Fine Point Calligraphy Brush Pens

- Fine Point Calligraphy Markers

Note: The best writing tools will allow you to create both a thin upstroke and thick downstroke.  When learning calligraphy, experiment with a variety of writing tools to find which will work best for you.

ISBN-13:  978-1-64281-050-9

# Table of Contents

# Calligraphy Practice Strokes

Following the starting arrows, trace the gray lines.
On the blank lines provided, copy the practice strokes.

## Thin Upstrokes

Use light pressure to form thin upstrokes.

## Thick Downstrokes

Use firm pressure to form thick downstrokes.

## Slant

Letters are written with a 55 degree slant.
Slanted lines are included as a guide to enable
you to achieve the proper letter slant.

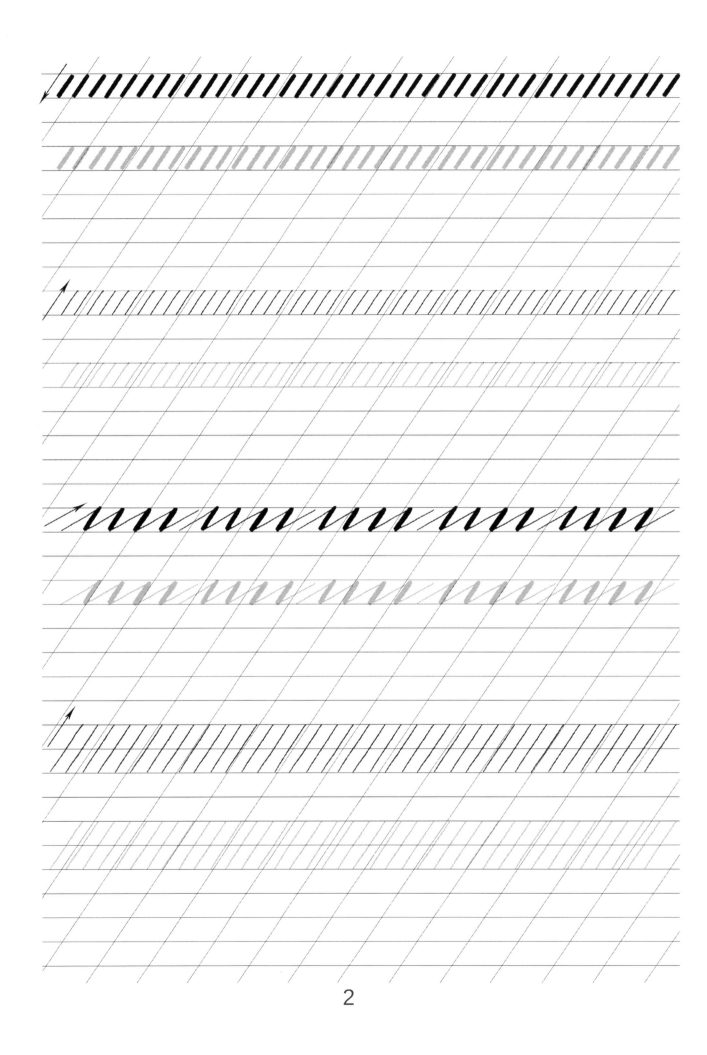

2

3

4

5

9

13

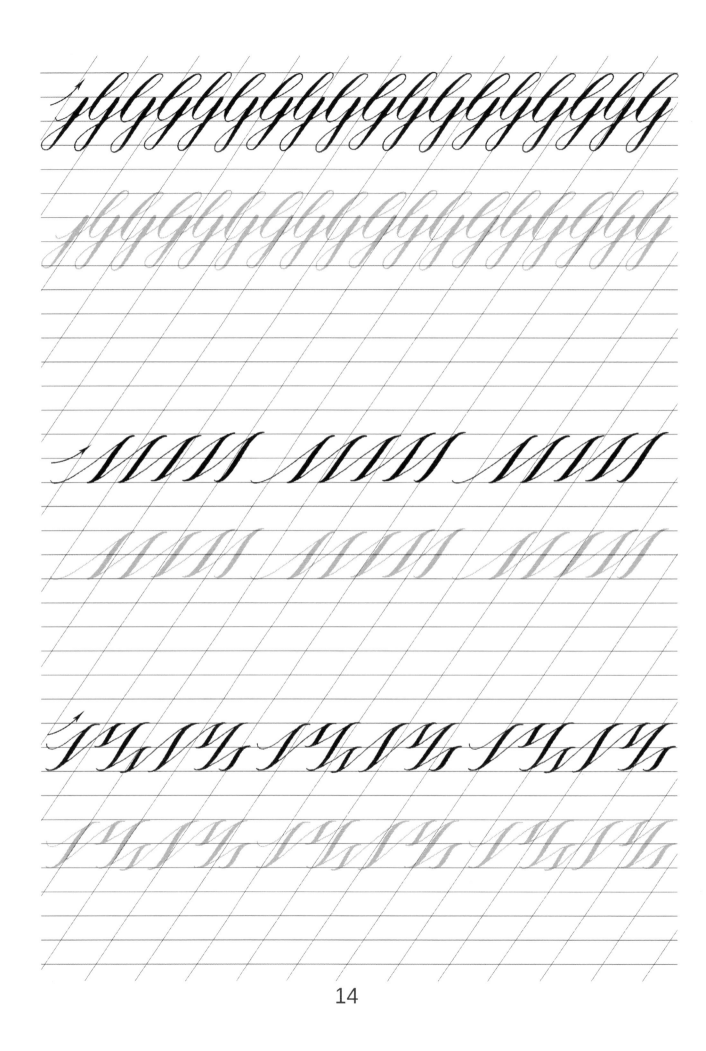

15

17

# Lowercase Letters

## Group I

i, t, u, j
n, m, r, p
v, w, y

## Group II

c, e, o, a
g, q, d

## Group III

b, l, h, k

## Group IV

f, z, x, s

Note: Baseline is the writing line.

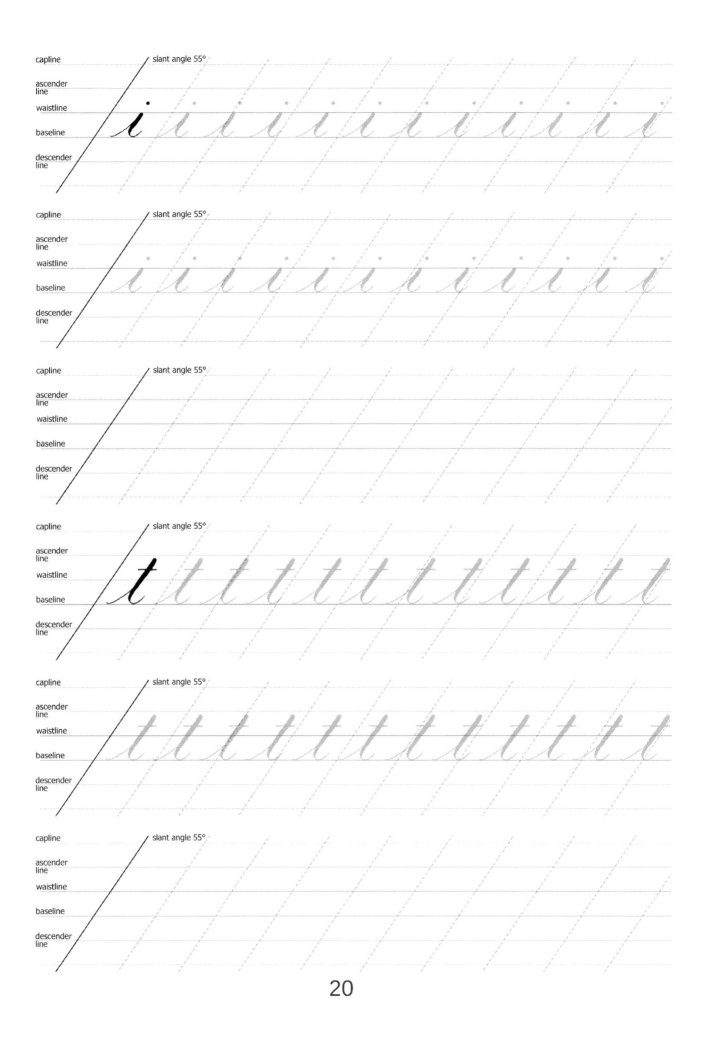

20

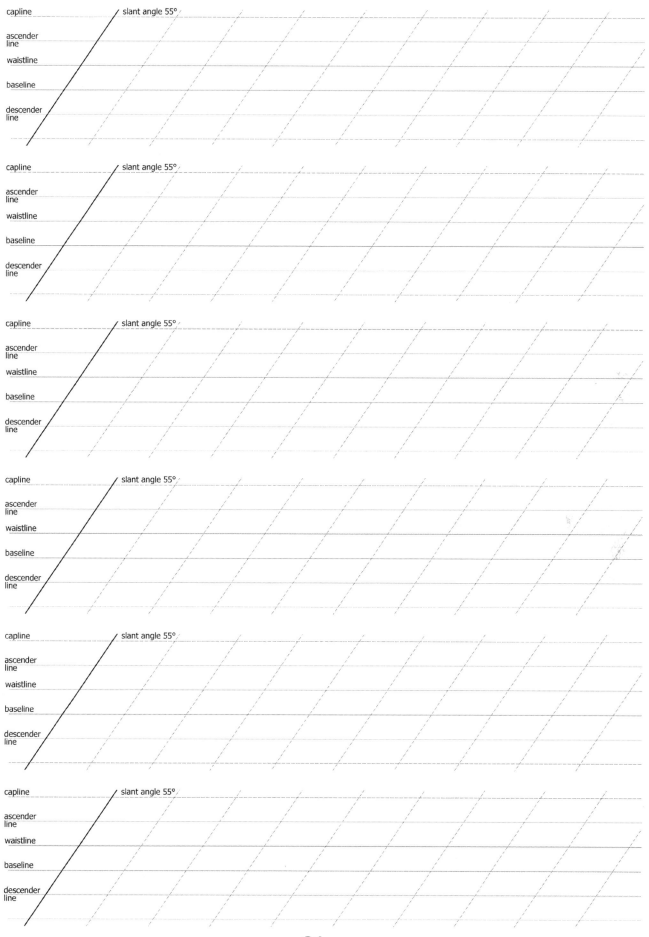

capline     slant angle 55°
ascender line
waistline
baseline
descender line

capline     slant angle 55°
ascender line
waistline
baseline
descender line

capline     slant angle 55°
ascender line
waistline
baseline
descender line

capline     slant angle 55°
ascender line
waistline
baseline
descender line

capline     slant angle 55°
ascender line
waistline
baseline
descender line

capline     slant angle 55°
ascender line
waistline
baseline
descender line

21

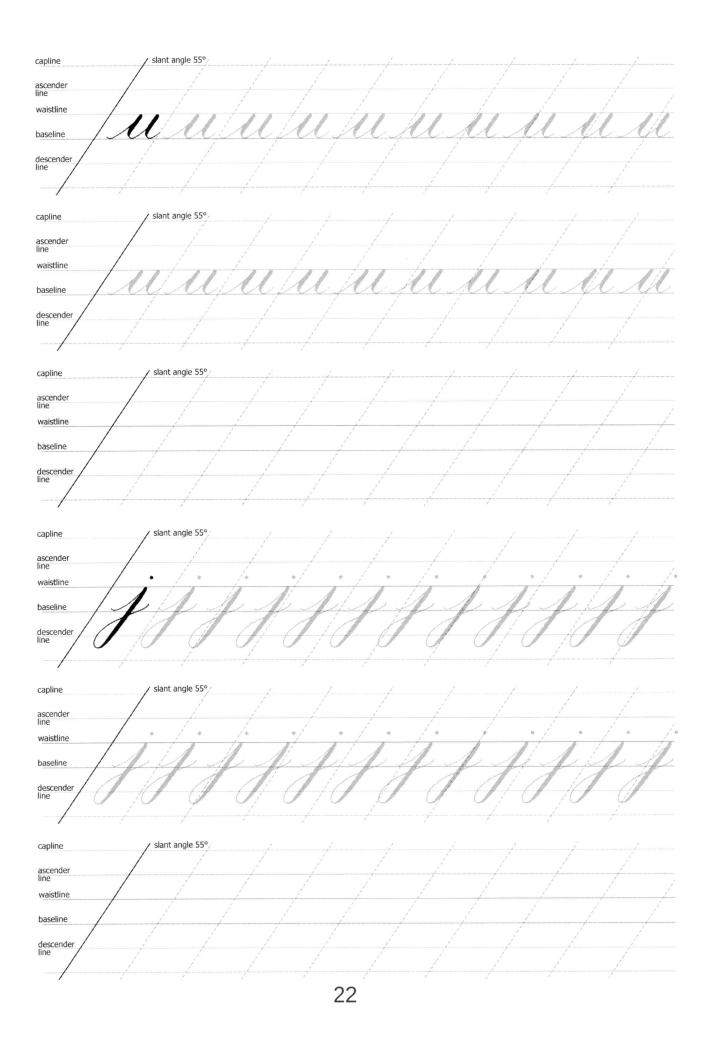

capline
ascender line
waistline
baseline
descender line
slant angle 55°

*u*

capline
ascender line
waistline
baseline
descender line
slant angle 55°

capline
ascender line
waistline
baseline
descender line
slant angle 55°

capline
ascender line
waistline
baseline
descender line
slant angle 55°

*j*

capline
ascender line
waistline
baseline
descender line
slant angle 55°

capline
ascender line
waistline
baseline
descender line
slant angle 55°

22

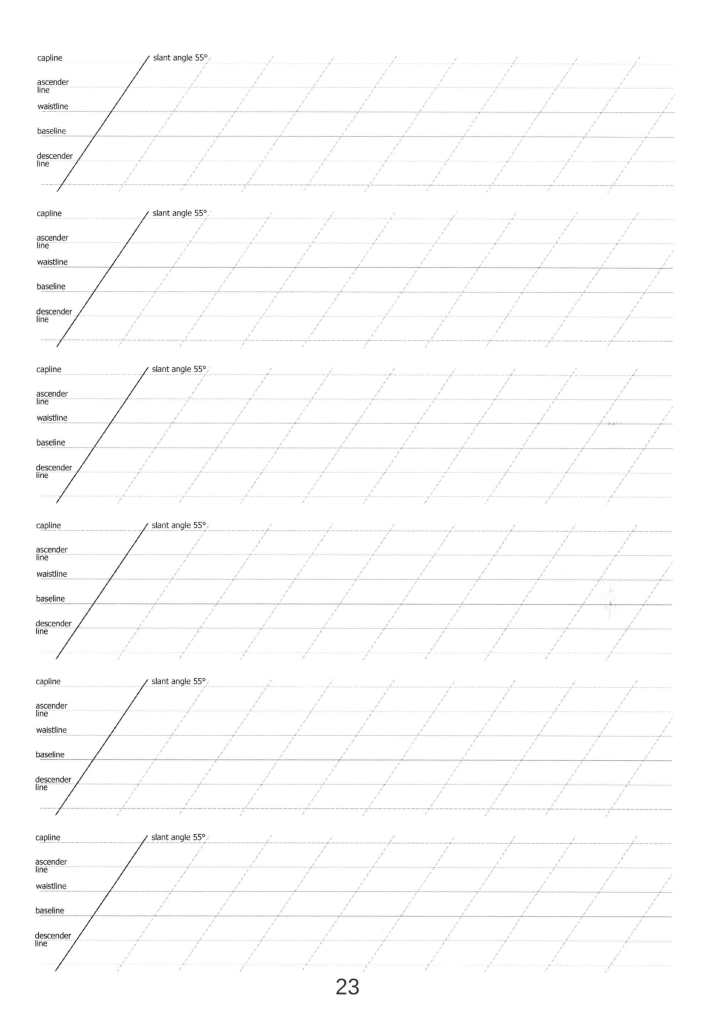

capline
slant angle 55°
ascender line
waistline
baseline
descender line

capline
slant angle 55°
ascender line
waistline
baseline
descender line

capline
slant angle 55°
ascender line
waistline
baseline
descender line

capline
slant angle 55°
ascender line
waistline
baseline
descender line

capline
slant angle 55°
ascender line
waistline
baseline
descender line

capline
slant angle 55°
ascender line
waistline
baseline
descender line

23

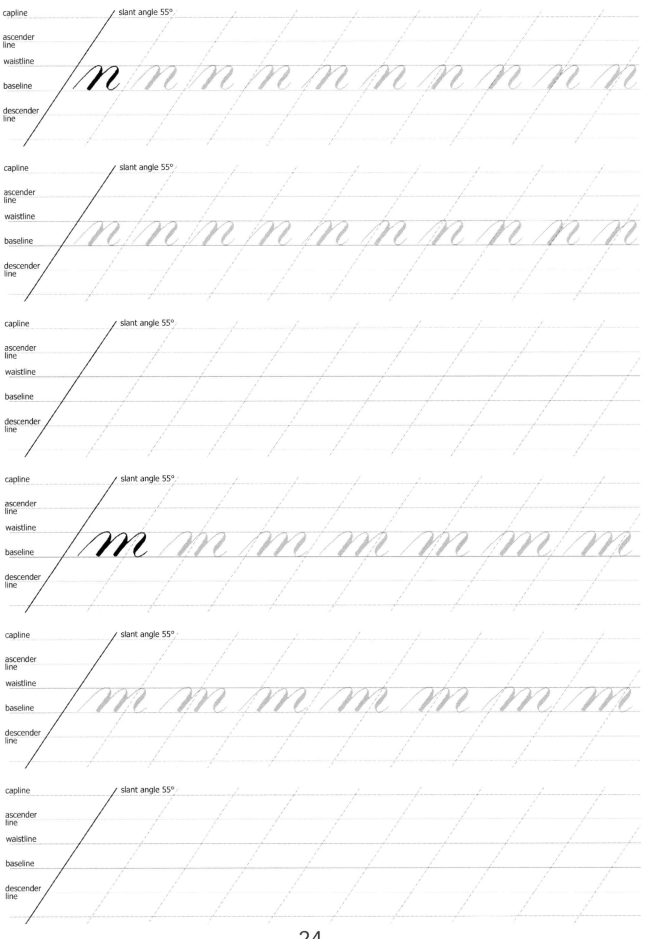

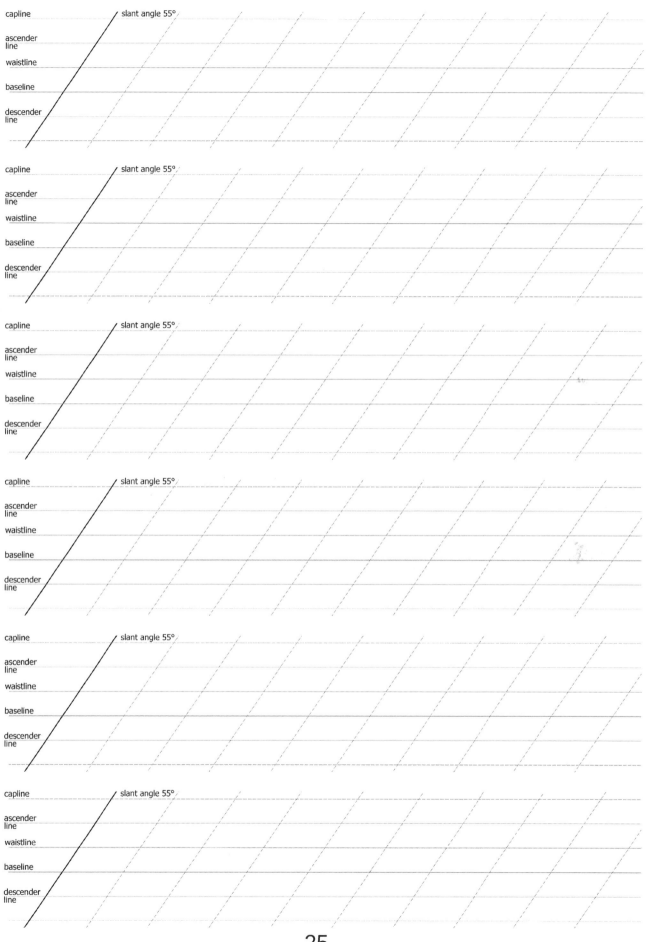

capline     slant angle 55°
ascender line
waistline
baseline
descender line

capline     slant angle 55°
ascender line
waistline
baseline
descender line

capline     slant angle 55°
ascender line
waistline
baseline
descender line

capline     slant angle 55°
ascender line
waistline
baseline
descender line

capline     slant angle 55°
ascender line
waistline
baseline
descender line

capline     slant angle 55°
ascender line
waistline
baseline
descender line

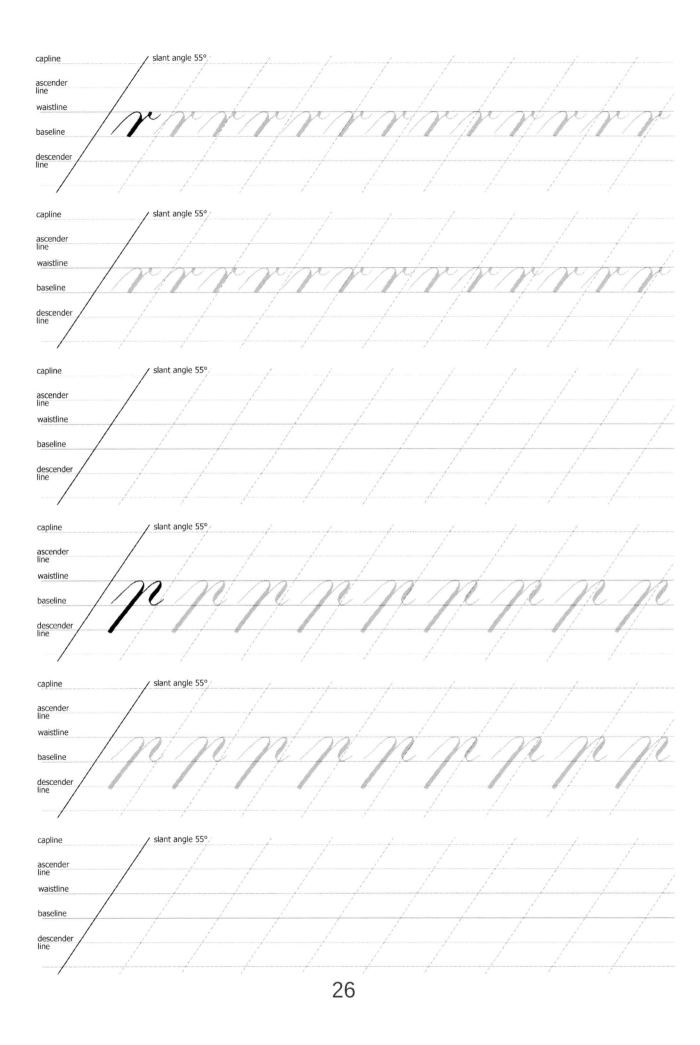

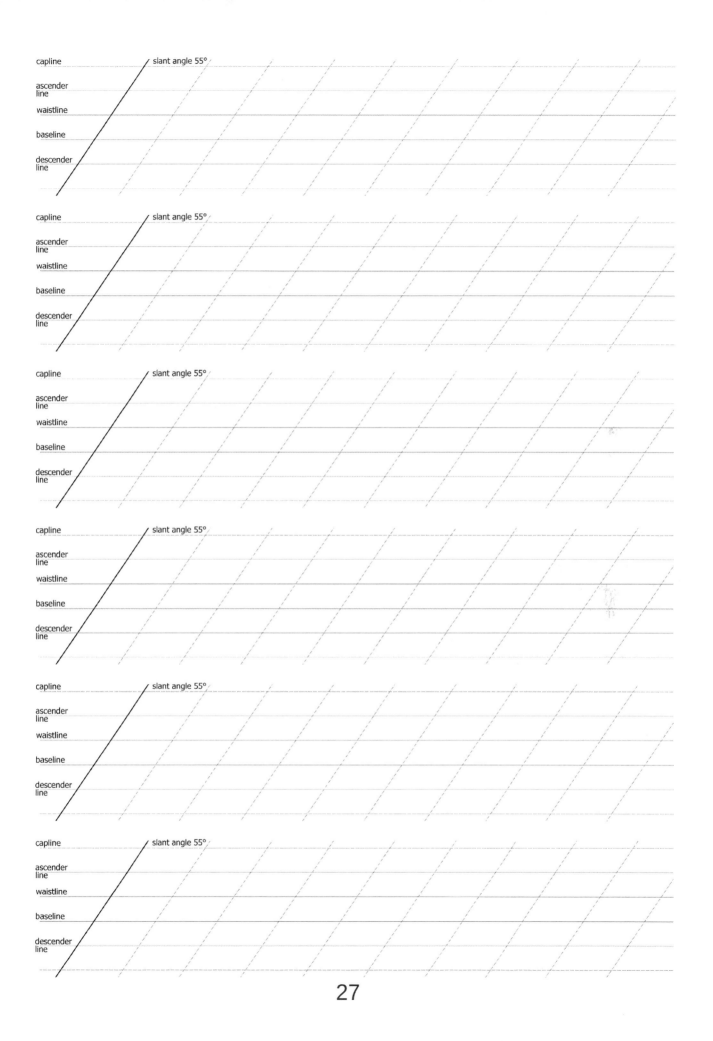

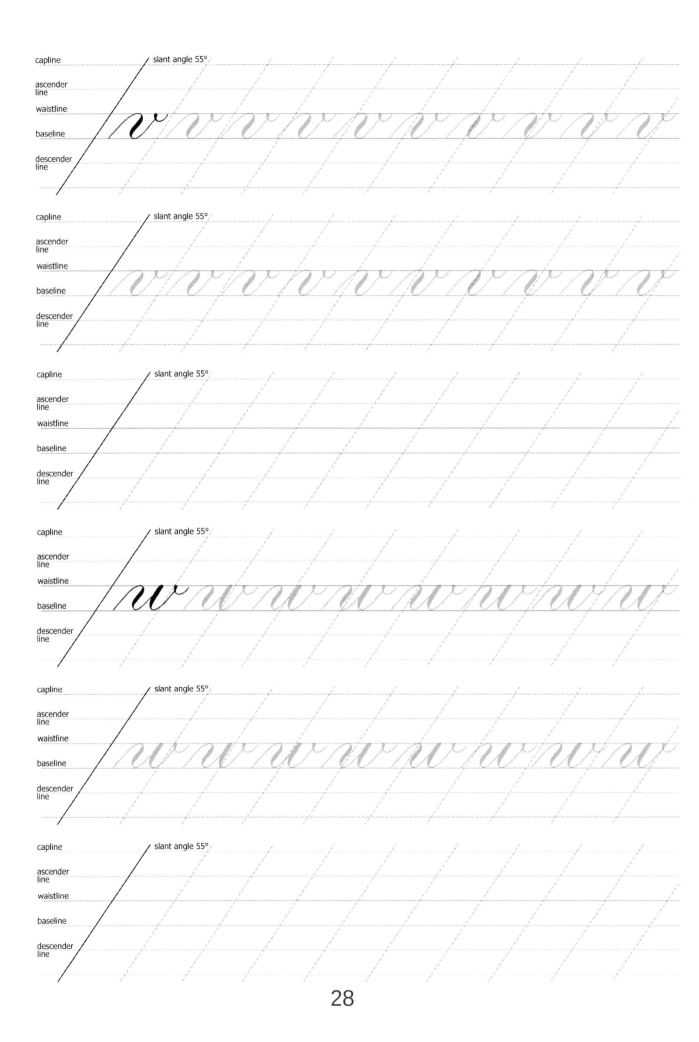

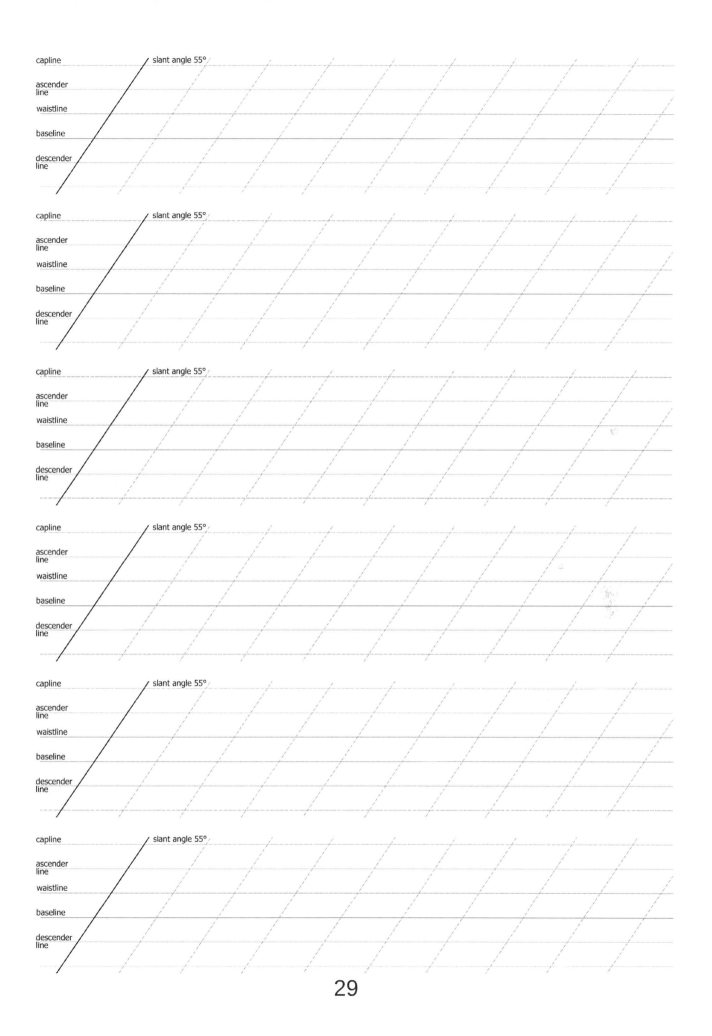

capline                    slant angle 55°
ascender
line
waistline
baseline
descender
line

capline                    slant angle 55°
ascender
line
waistline
baseline
descender
line

capline                    slant angle 55°
ascender
line
waistline
baseline
descender
line

capline                    slant angle 55°
ascender
line
waistline
baseline
descender
line

capline                    slant angle 55°
ascender
line
waistline
baseline
descender
line

capline                    slant angle 55°
ascender
line
waistline
baseline
descender
line

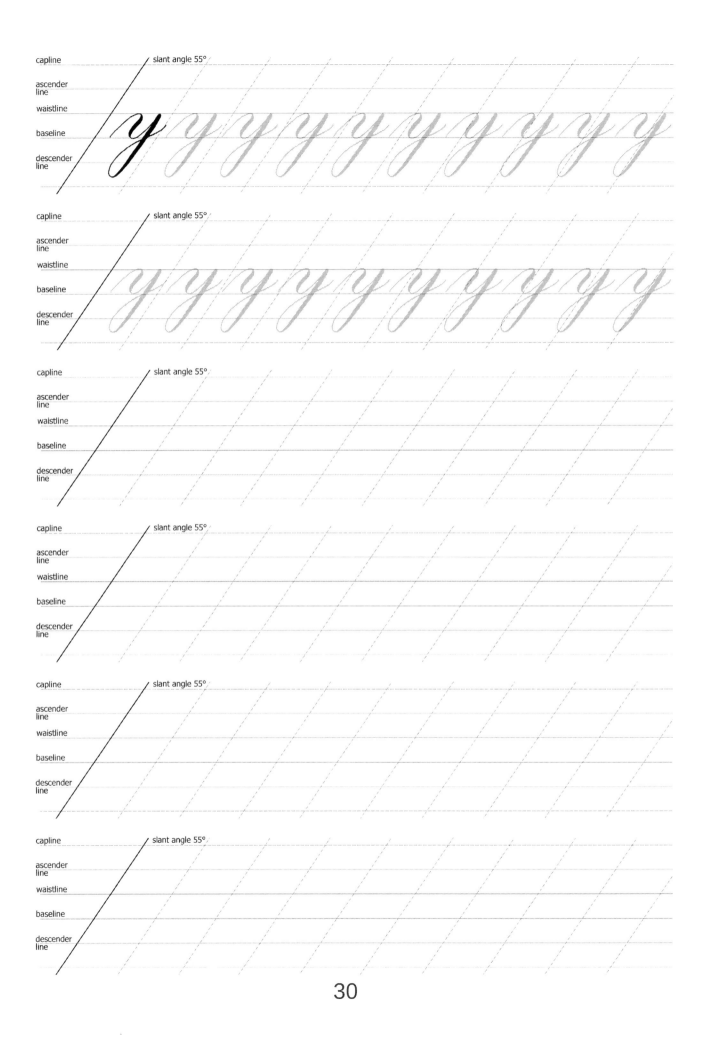

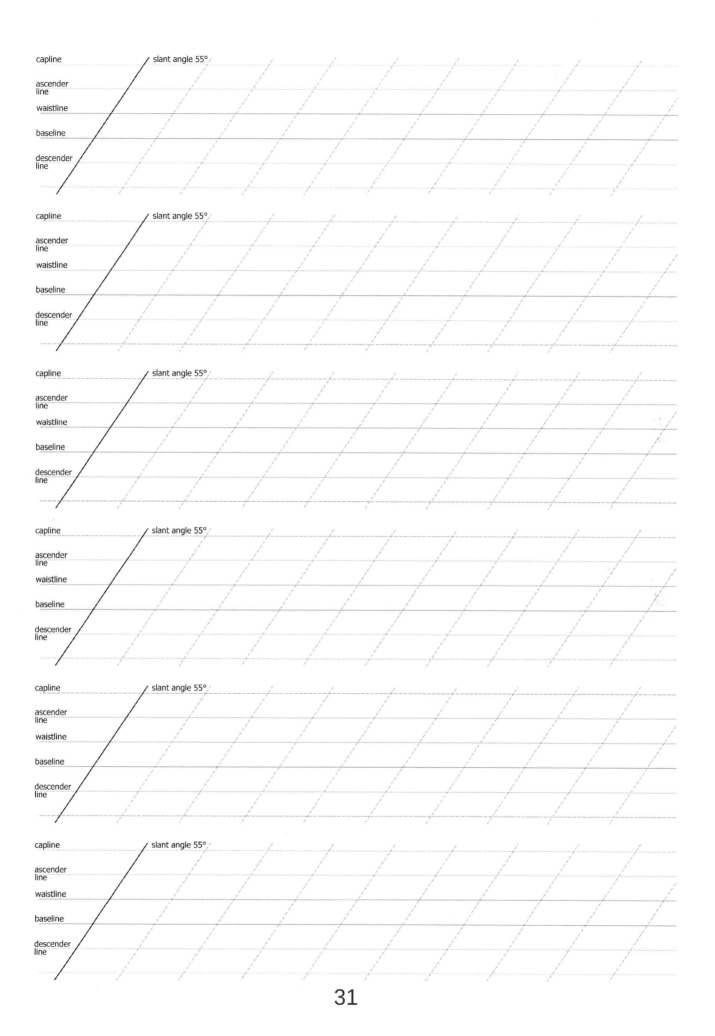

31

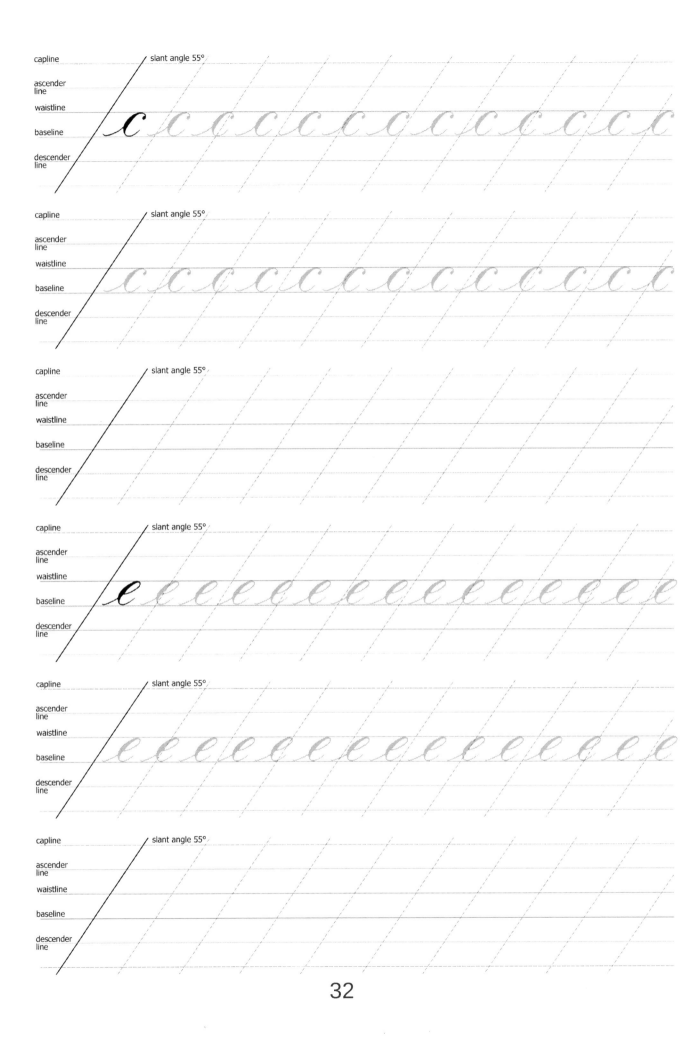

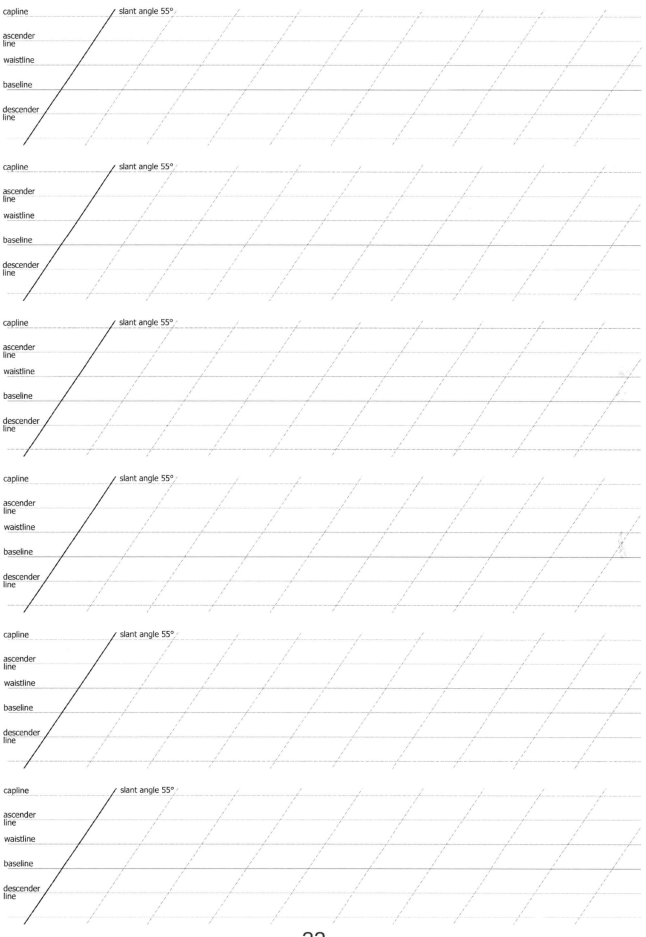

33

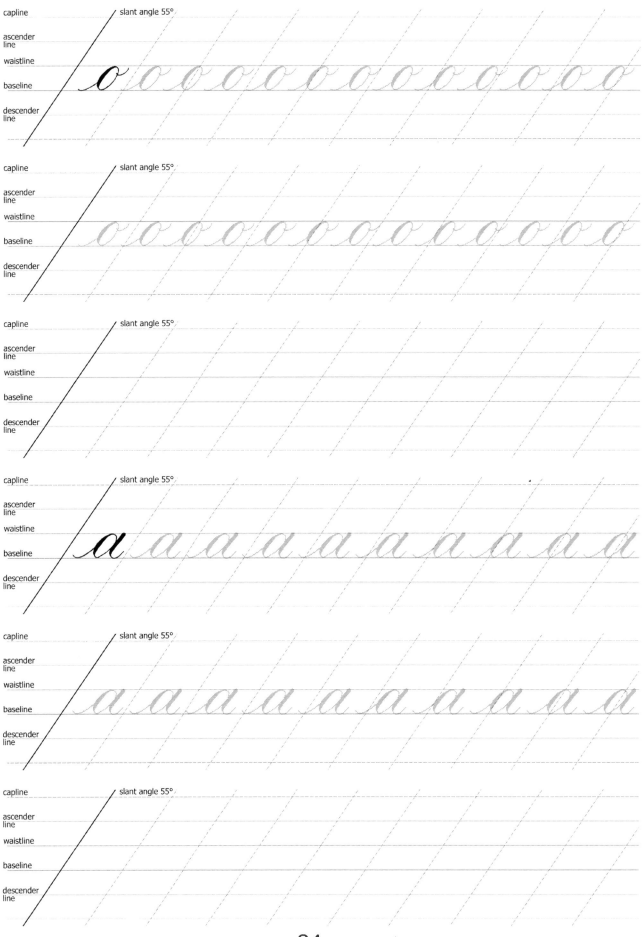

34

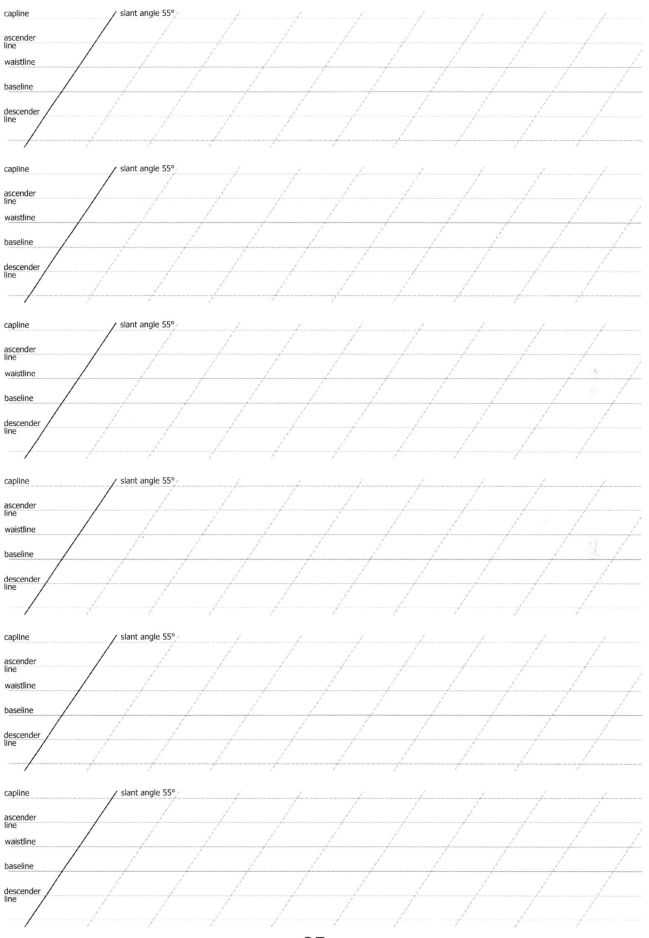

capline

ascender line

waistline

baseline

descender line

slant angle 55°

capline

ascender line

waistline

baseline

descender line

slant angle 55°

capline

ascender line

waistline

baseline

descender line

slant angle 55°

capline

ascender line

waistline

baseline

descender line

slant angle 55°

capline

ascender line

waistline

baseline

descender line

slant angle 55°

capline

ascender line

waistline

baseline

descender line

slant angle 55°

35

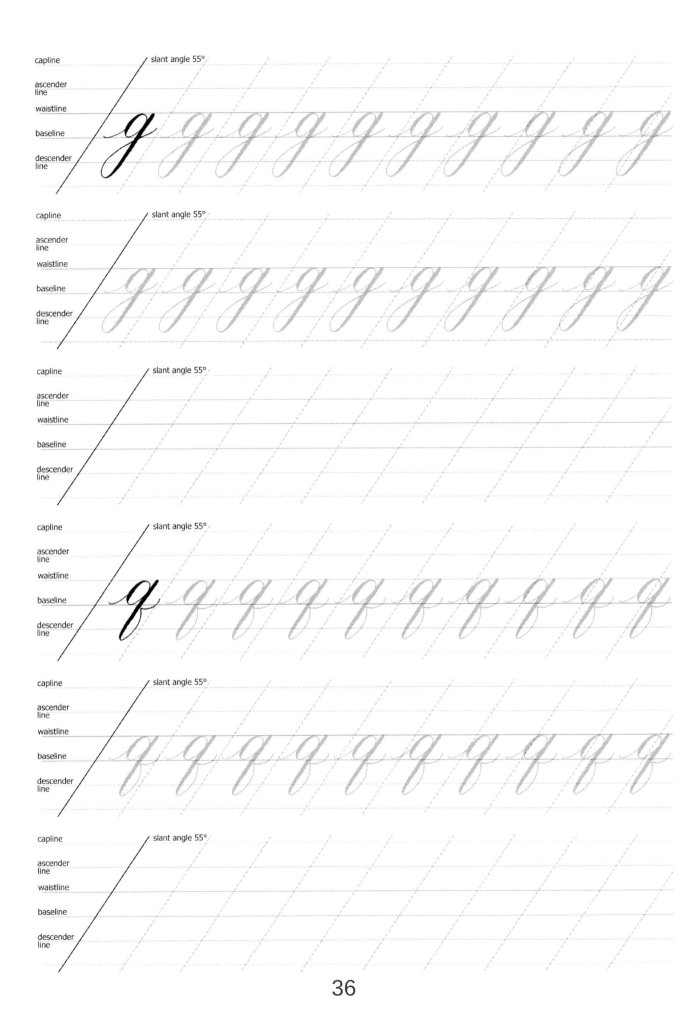

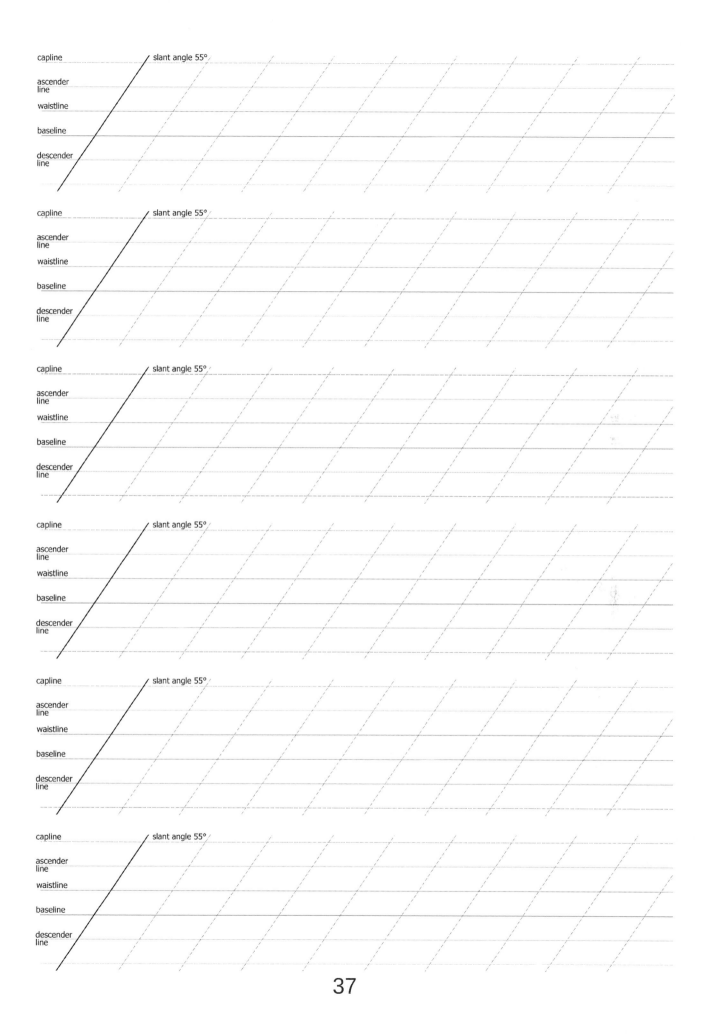

37

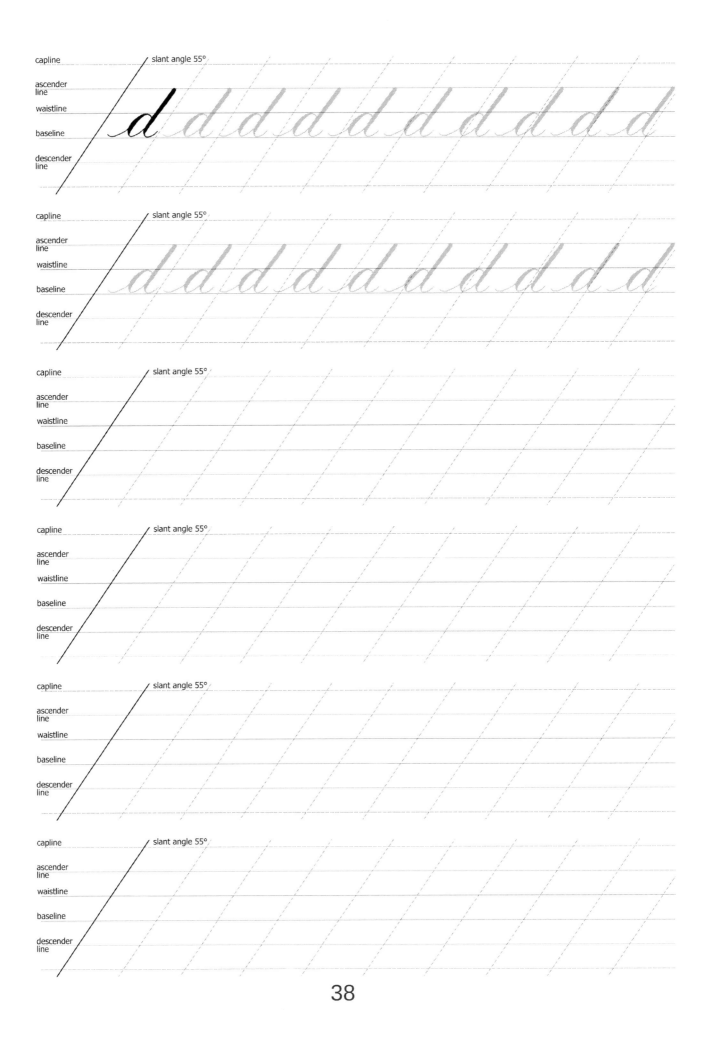

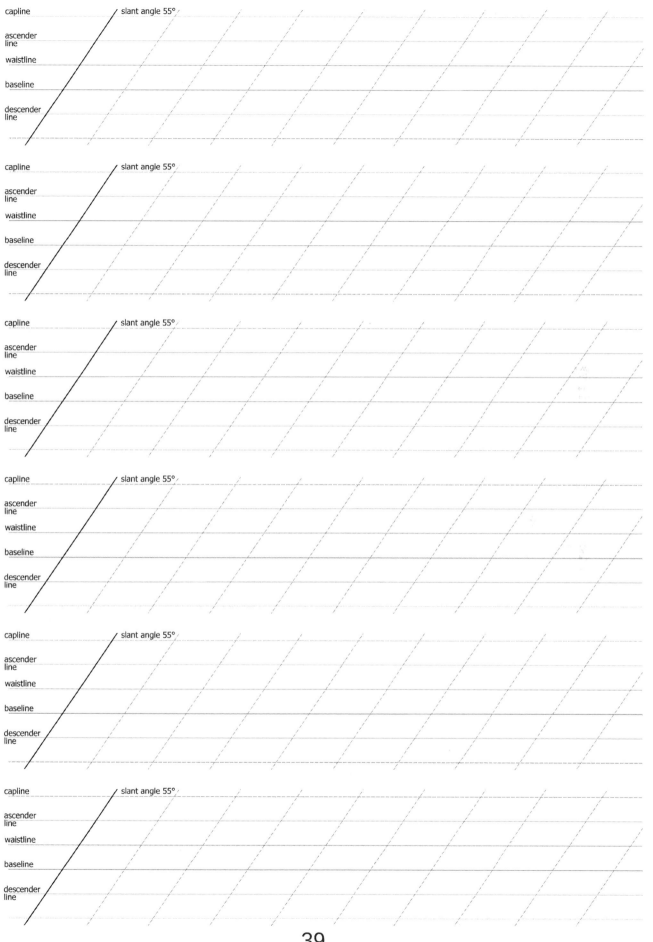

capline

slant angle 55°

ascender
line

waistline

baseline

descender
line

capline

slant angle 55°

ascender
line

waistline

baseline

descender
line

capline

slant angle 55°

ascender
line

waistline

baseline

descender
line

capline

slant angle 55°

ascender
line

waistline

baseline

descender
line

capline

slant angle 55°

ascender
line

waistline

baseline

descender
line

capline

slant angle 55°

ascender
line

waistline

baseline

descender
line

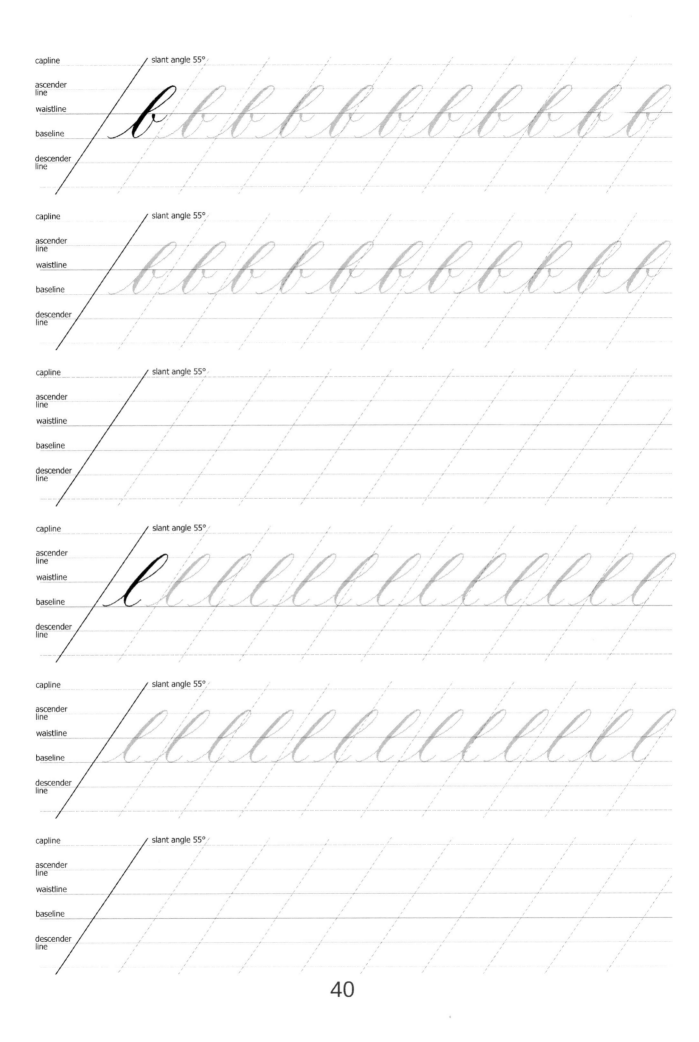

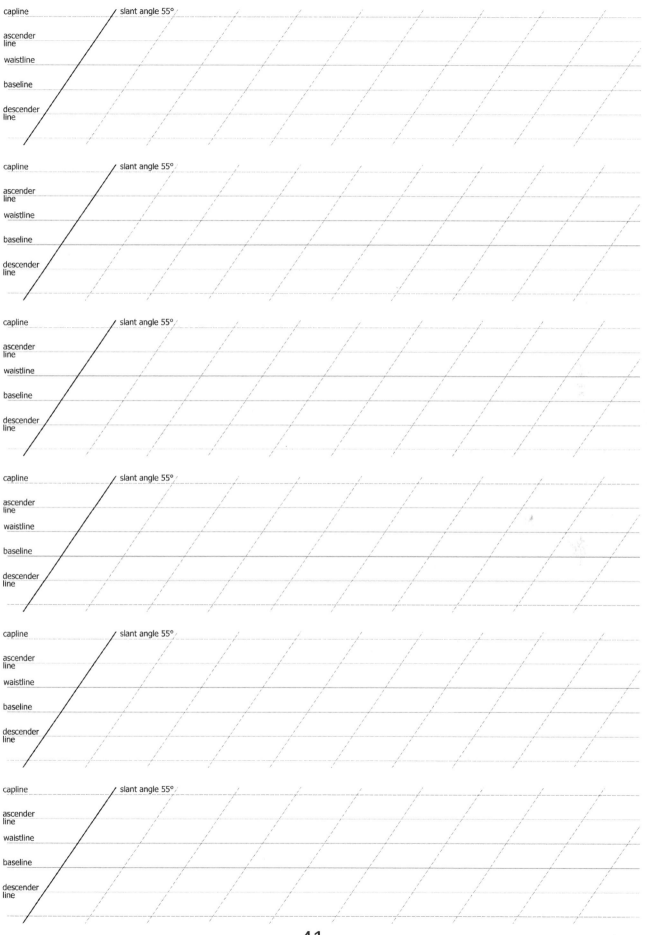

capline
ascender line
waistline
baseline
descender line

slant angle 55°

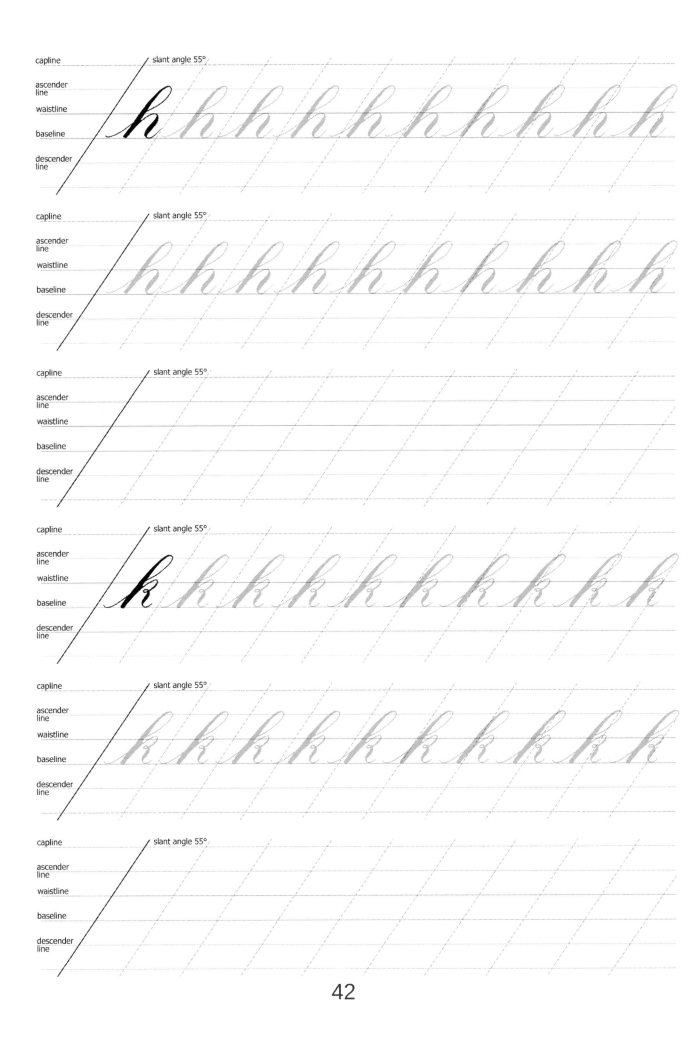

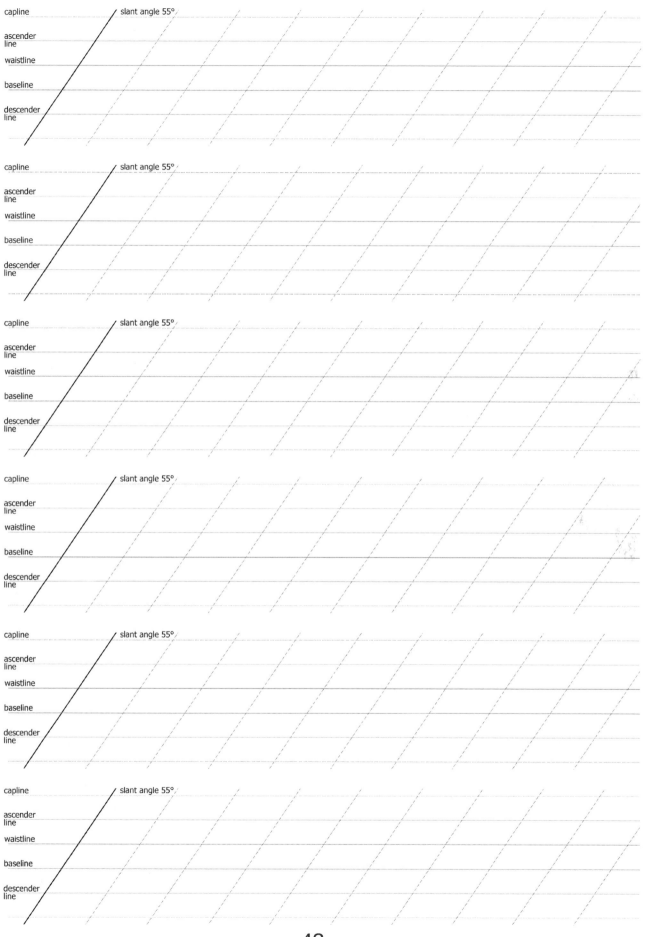

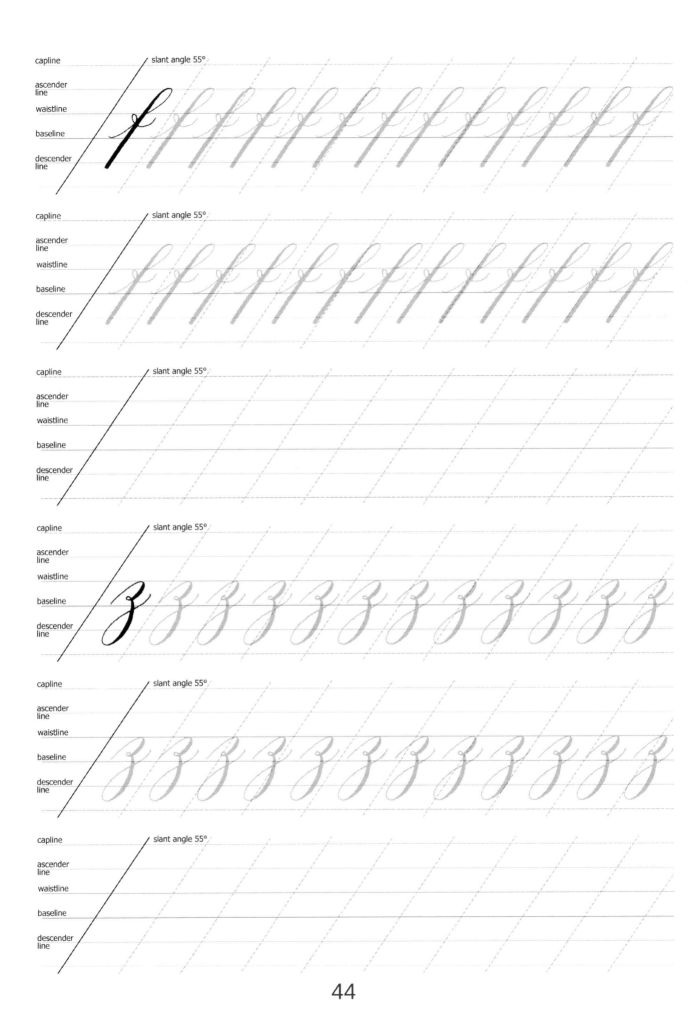

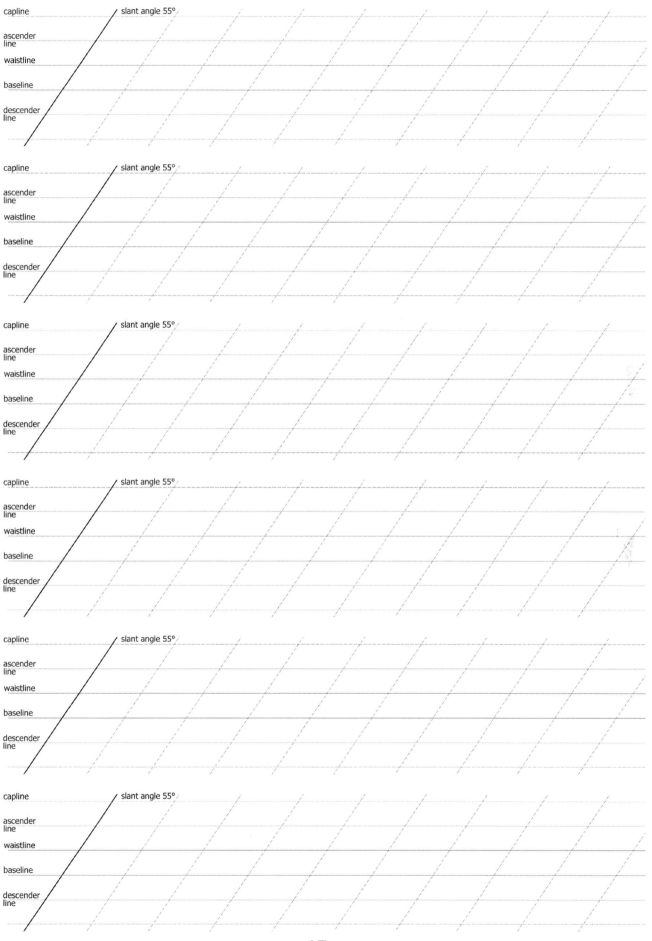

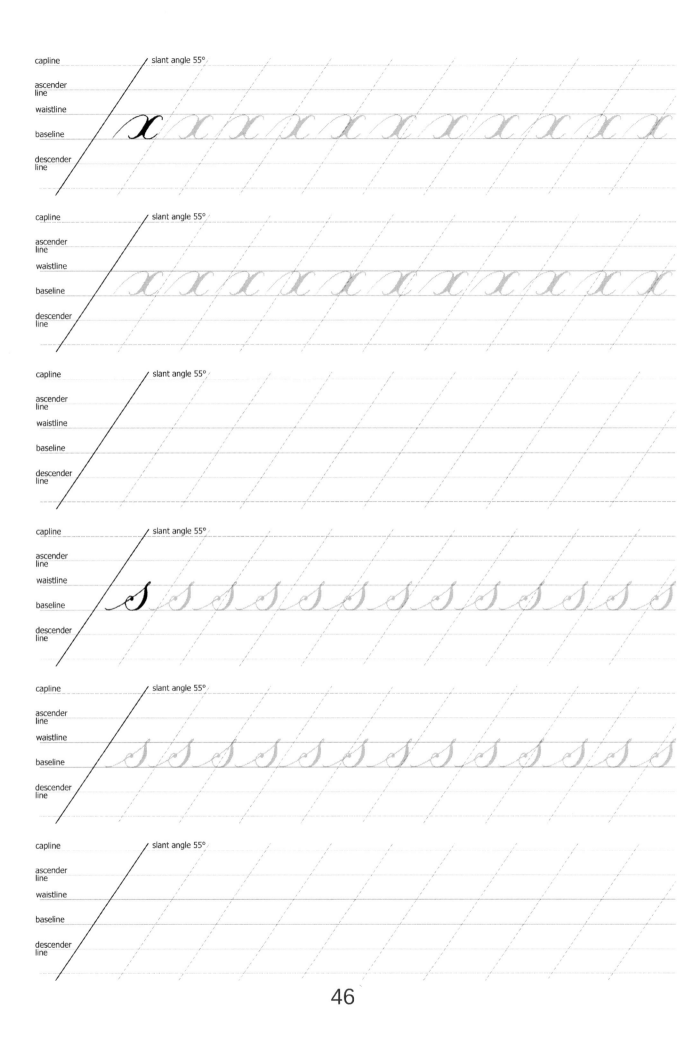

46

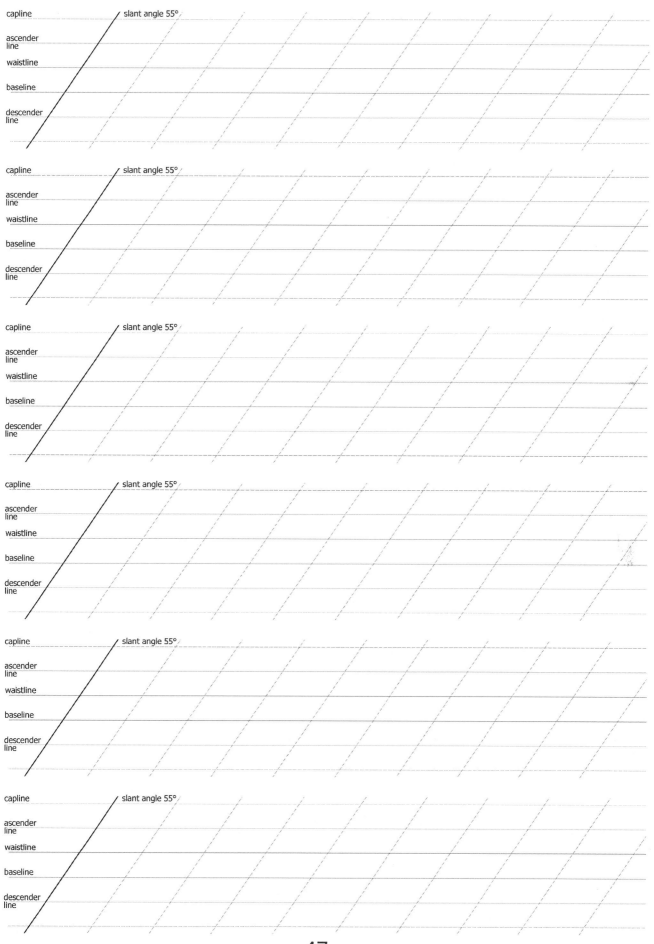

# Combining Letters

# Writing Words

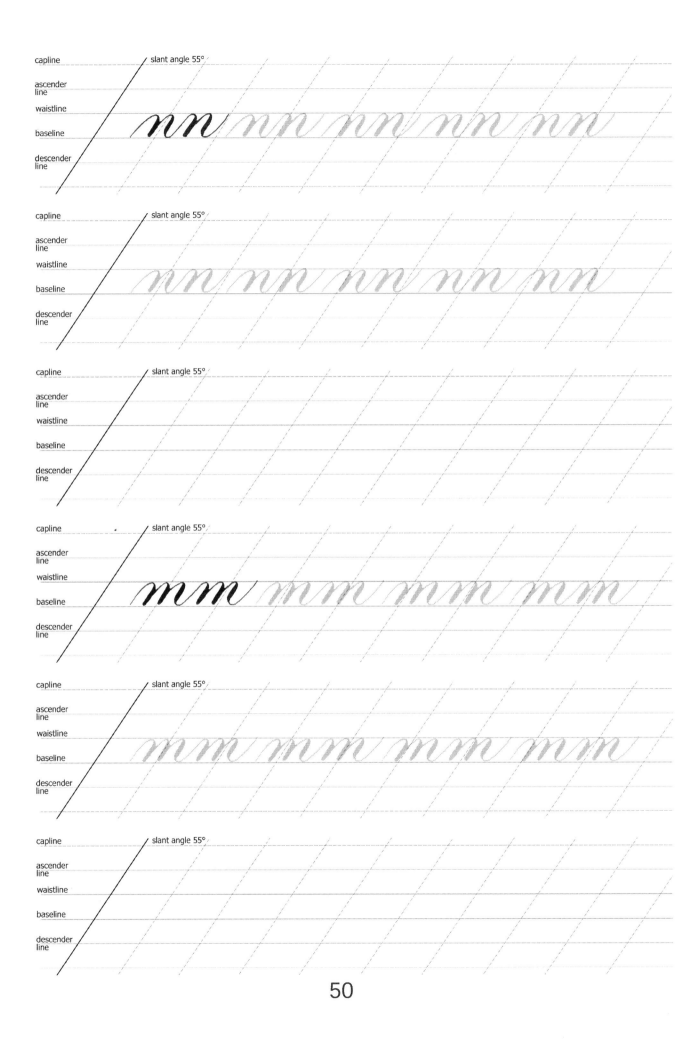

50

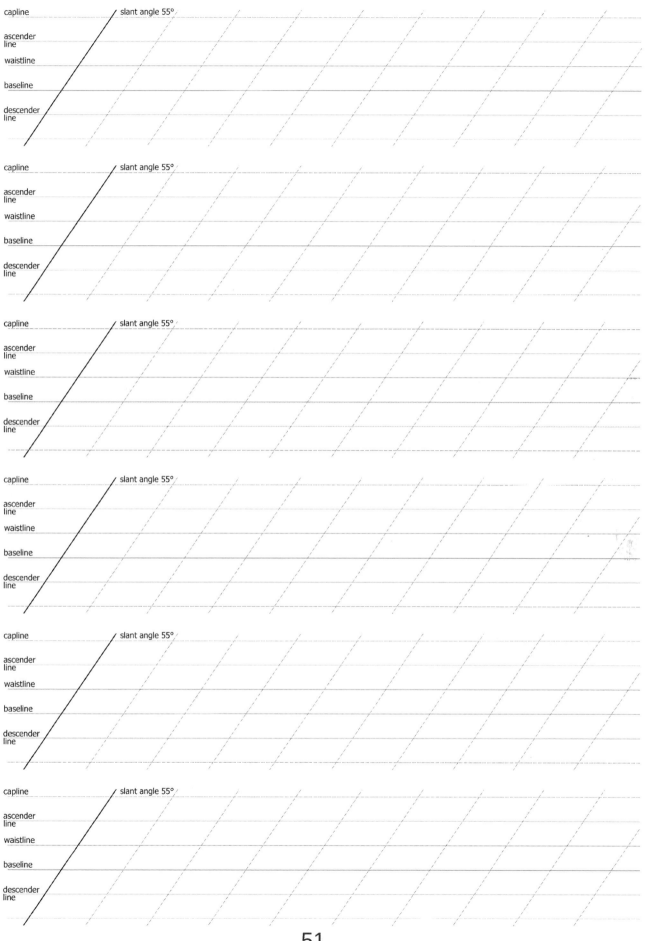

capline  slant angle 55°
ascender line
waistline
baseline
descender line

capline  slant angle 55°
ascender line
waistline
baseline
descender line

capline  slant angle 55°
ascender line
waistline
baseline
descender line

capline  slant angle 55°
ascender line
waistline
baseline
descender line

capline  slant angle 55°
ascender line
waistline
baseline
descender line

capline  slant angle 55°
ascender line
waistline
baseline
descender line

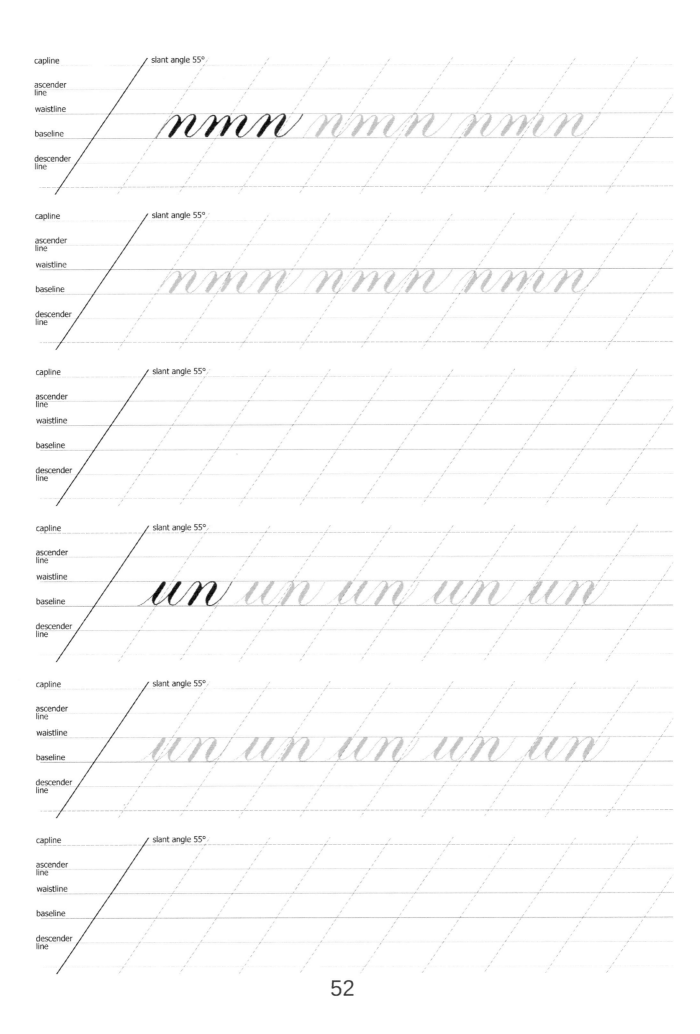

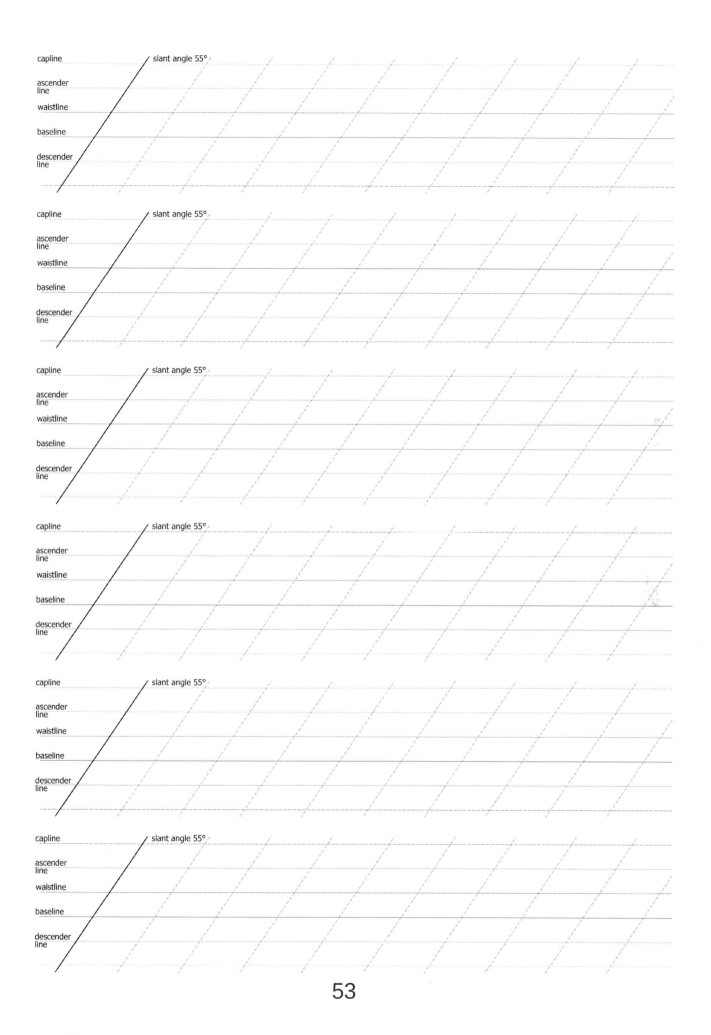

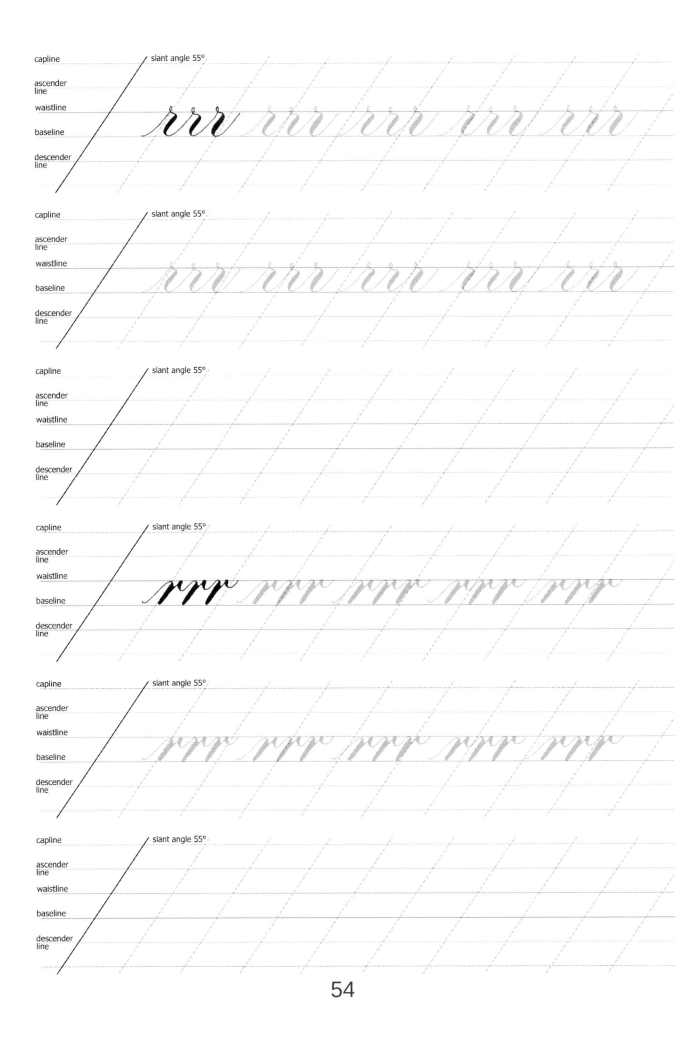

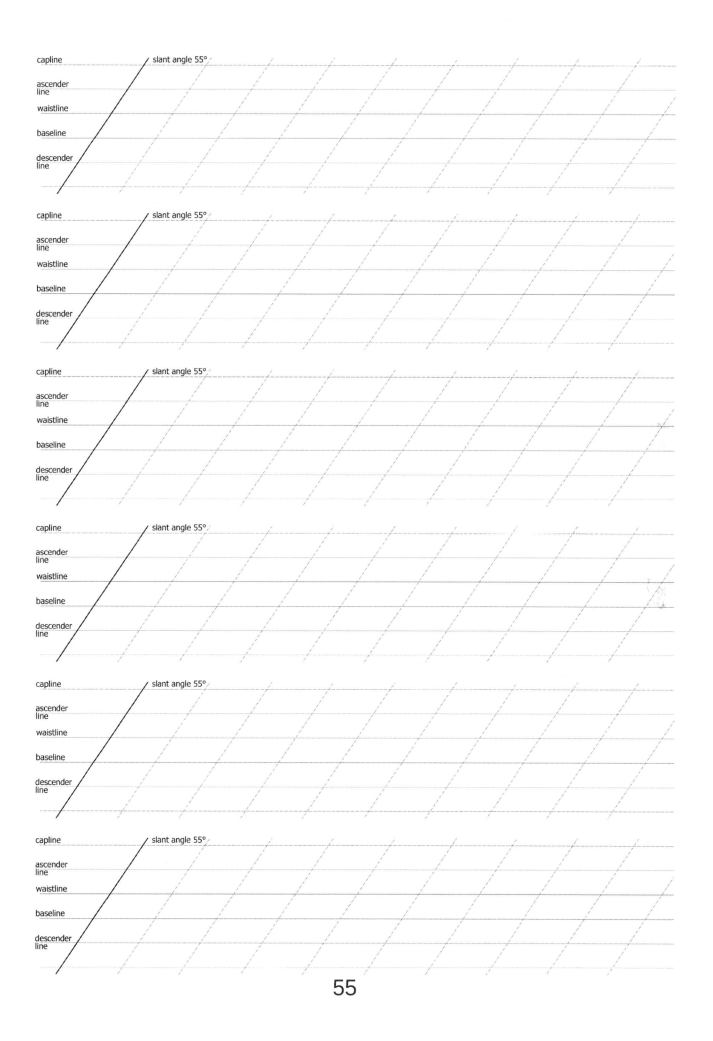

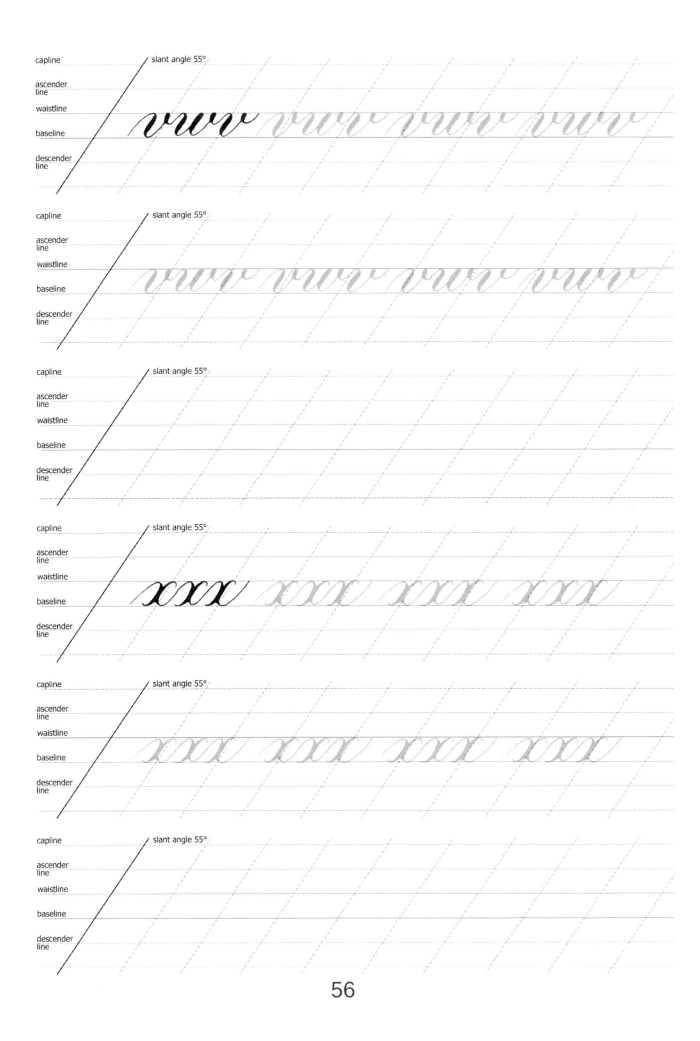

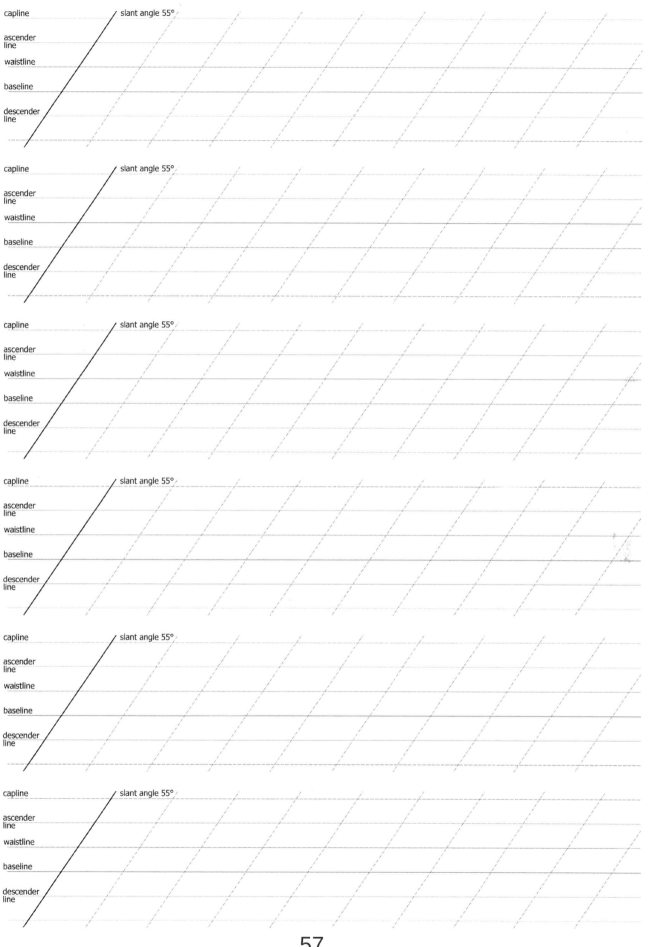

capline
ascender line
waistline
baseline
descender line

slant angle 55°

57

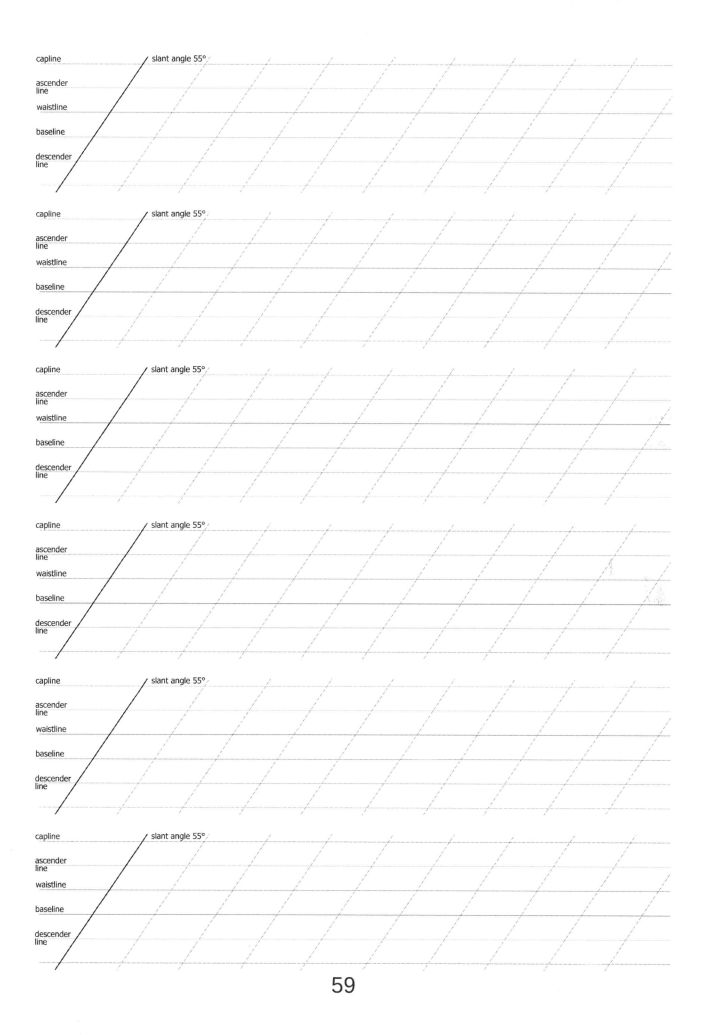

capline
ascender line
waistline
baseline
descender line
slant angle 55°

capline
ascender line
waistline
baseline
descender line
slant angle 55°

capline
ascender line
waistline
baseline
descender line
slant angle 55°

capline
ascender line
waistline
baseline
descender line
slant angle 55°

capline
ascender line
waistline
baseline
descender line
slant angle 55°

capline
ascender line
waistline
baseline
descender line
slant angle 55°

59

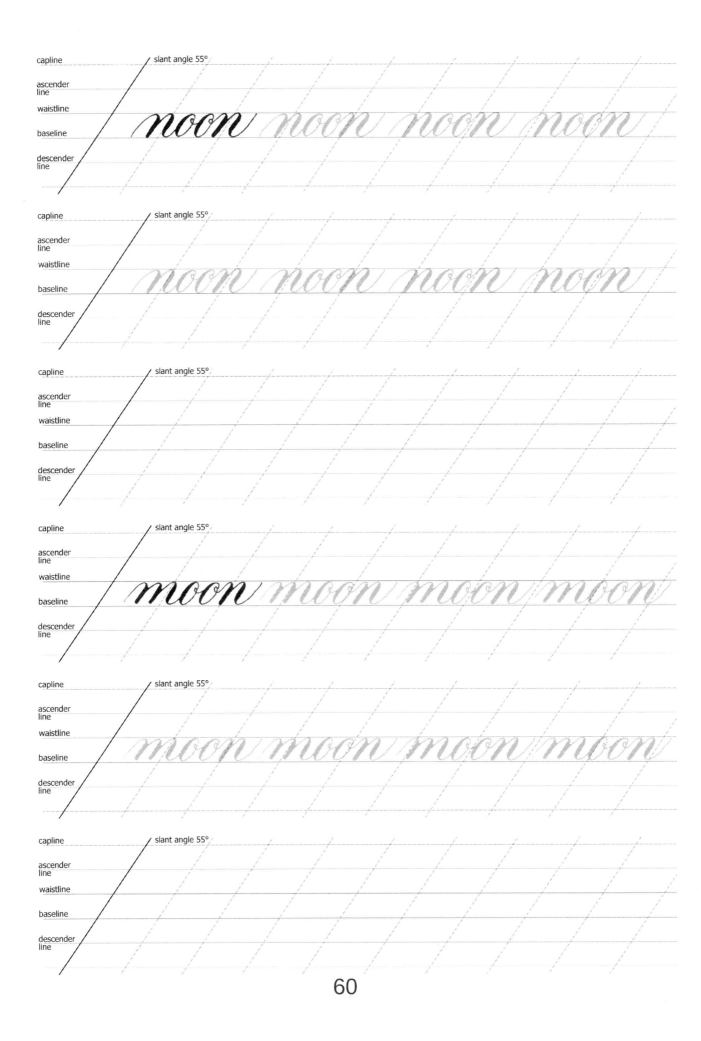

capline
ascender line
waistline
baseline
descender line

slant angle 55°

*noon noon noon noon*

capline
ascender line
waistline
baseline
descender line

slant angle 55°

*noon noon noon noon*

capline
ascender line
waistline
baseline
descender line

slant angle 55°

capline
ascender line
waistline
baseline
descender line

slant angle 55°

*moon moon moon moon*

capline
ascender line
waistline
baseline
descender line

slant angle 55°

*moon moon moon moon*

capline
ascender line
waistline
baseline
descender line

slant angle 55°

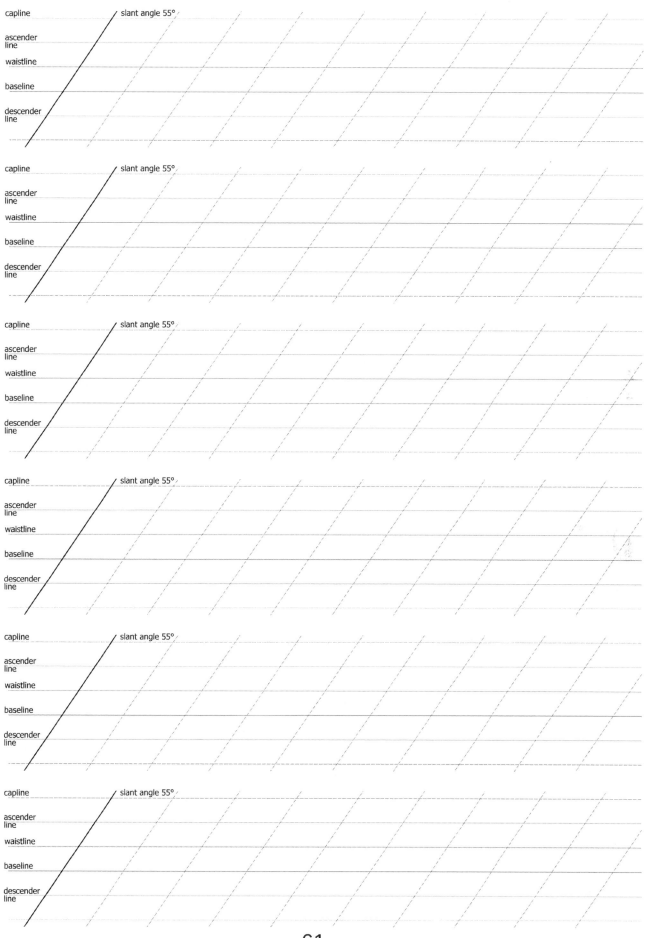

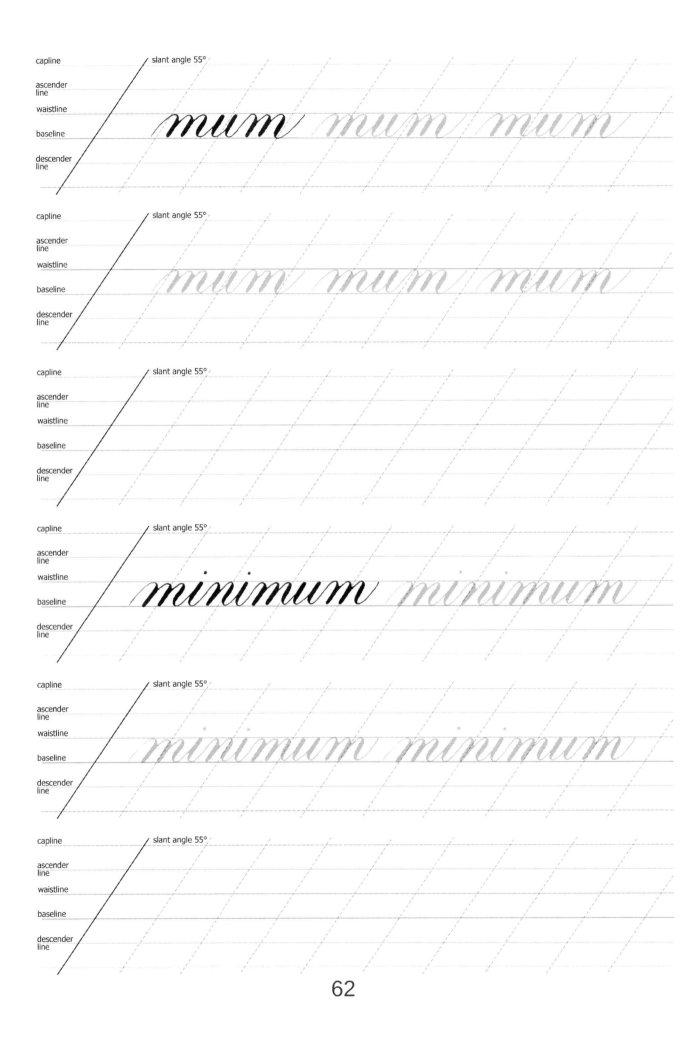

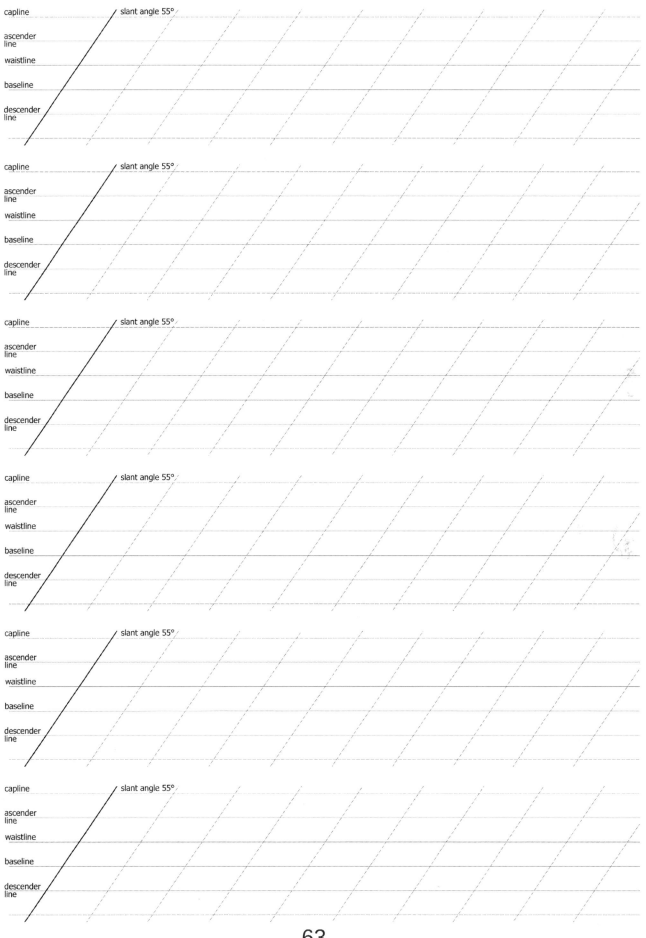

capline    slant angle 55°

ascender
line

waistline

baseline

descender
line

capline    slant angle 55°

ascender
line

waistline

baseline

descender
line

capline    slant angle 55°

ascender
line

waistline

baseline

descender
line

capline    slant angle 55°

ascender
line

waistline

baseline

descender
line

capline    slant angle 55°

ascender
line

waistline

baseline

descender
line

capline    slant angle 55°

ascender
line

waistline

baseline

descender
line

63

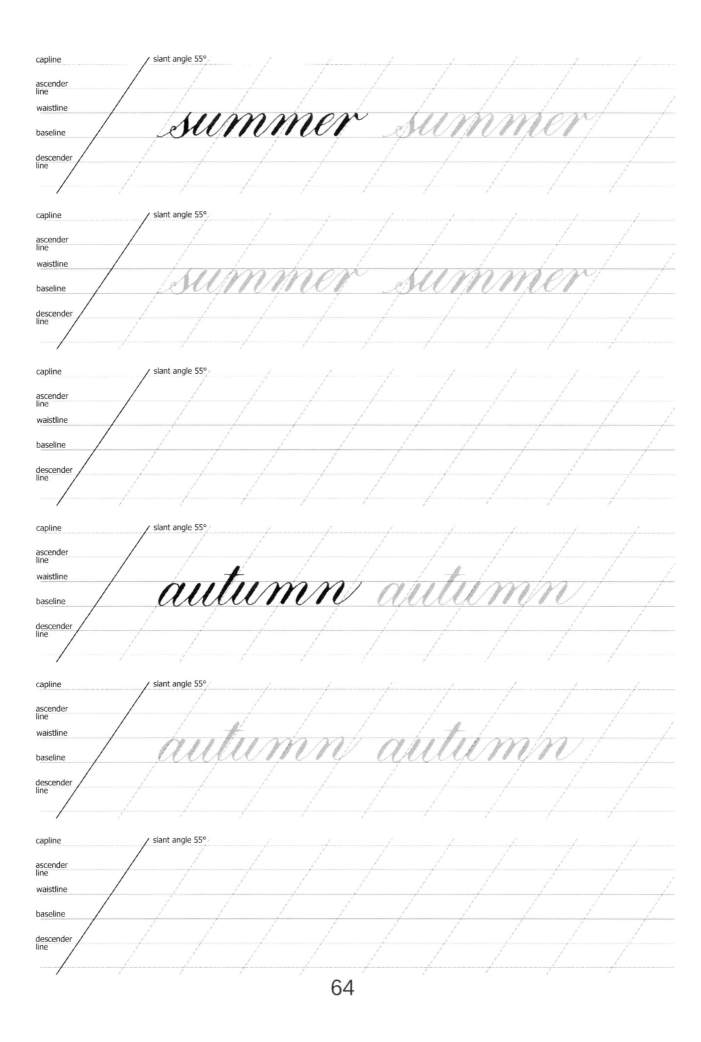

capline
ascender line
waistline
baseline
descender line
slant angle 55°

*summer* *summer* *summer*

*summer* *summer* *summer*

*autumn* *autumn* *autumn*

*autumn* *autumn*

64

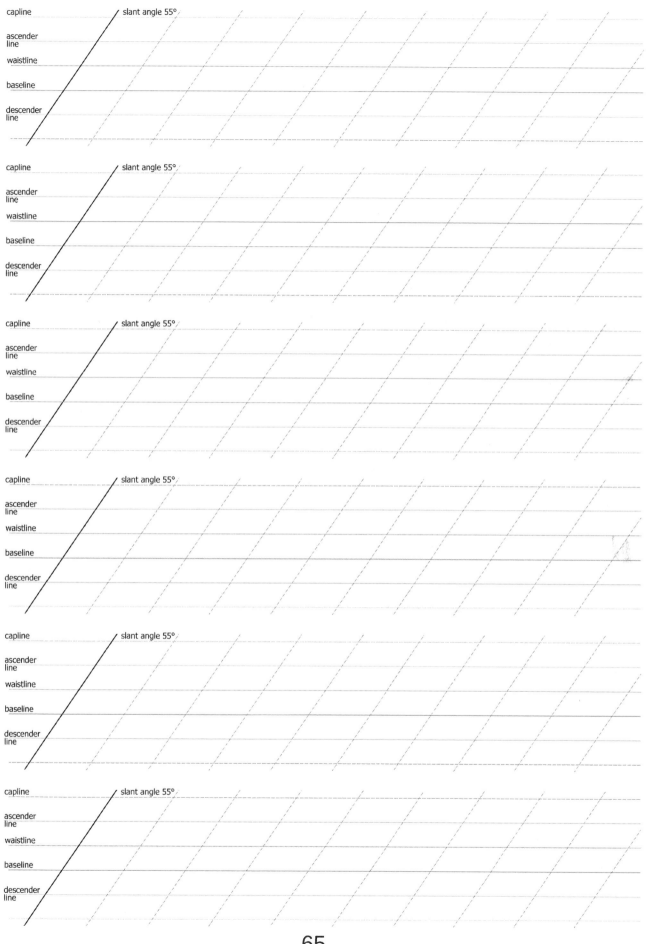

capline

ascender line

waistline

baseline

descender line

slant angle 55°

capline

ascender line

waistline

baseline

descender line

slant angle 55°

capline

ascender line

waistline

baseline

descender line

slant angle 55°

capline

ascender line

waistline

baseline

descender line

slant angle 55°

capline

ascender line

waistline

baseline

descender line

slant angle 55°

capline

ascender line

waistline

baseline

descender line

slant angle 55°

65

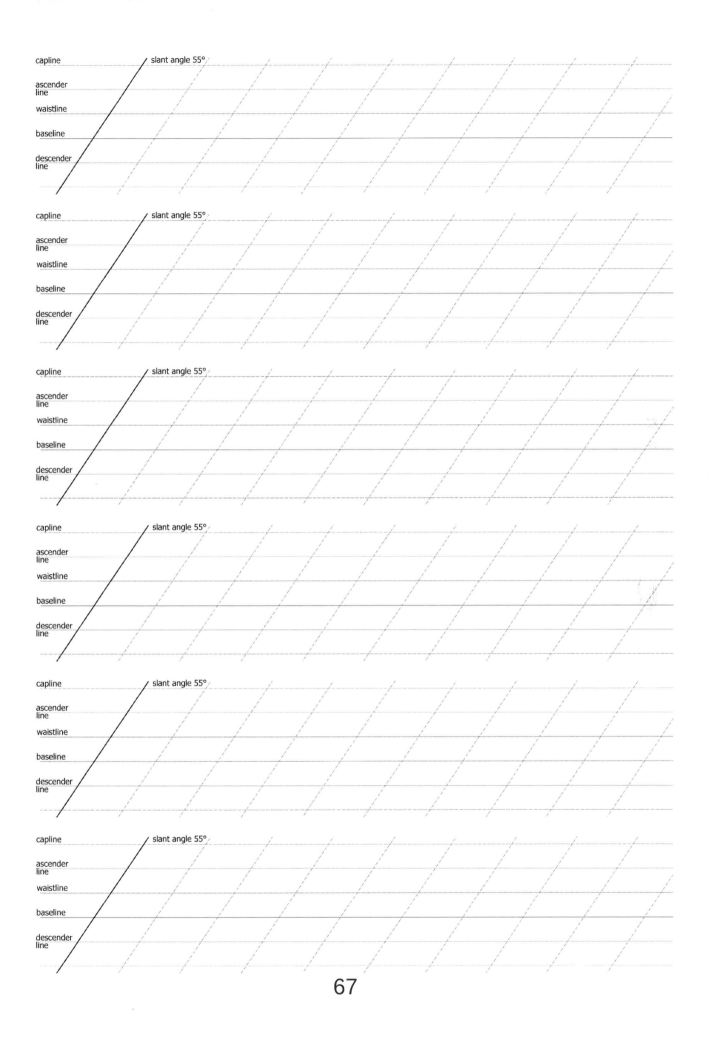

slant angle 55°

ascender
line

waistline

baseline

descender
line

*cocoa* cocoa cocoa cocoa

capline

slant angle 55°

ascender
line

waistline

baseline

descender
line

cocoa cocoa cocoa cocoa

capline

slant angle 55°

ascender
line

waistline

baseline

descender
line

capline

slant angle 55°

ascender
line

waistline

baseline

descender
line

*cinnamon* cinnamon

capline

slant angle 55°

ascender
line

waistline

baseline

descender
line

cinnamon cinnamon

capline

slant angle 55°

ascender
line

waistline

baseline

descender
line

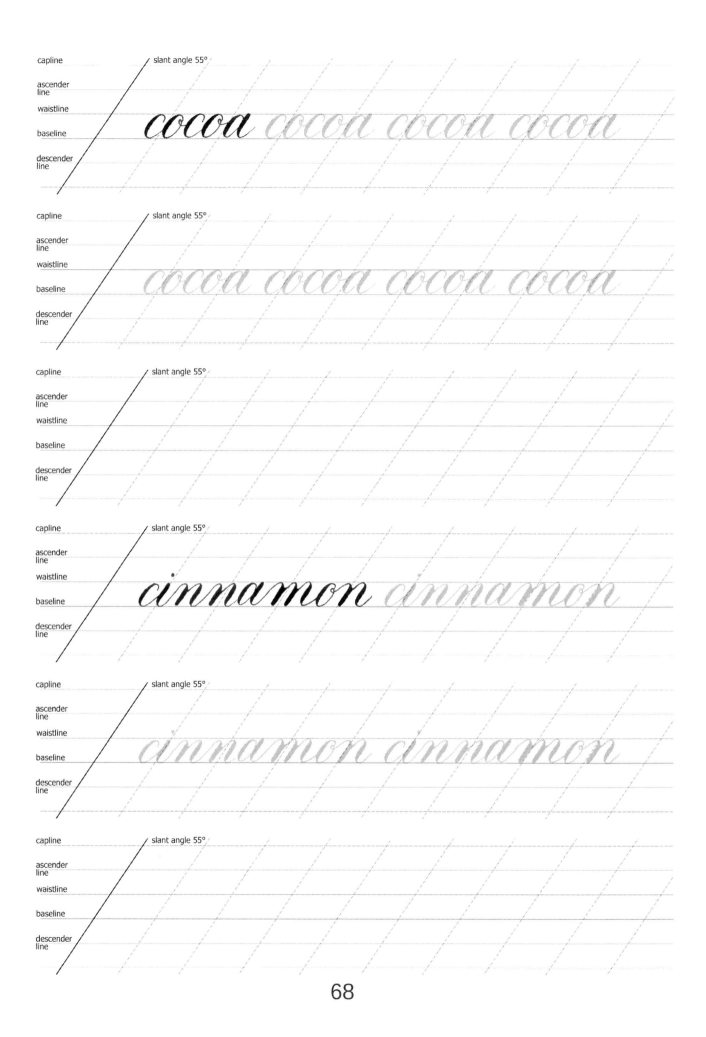

68

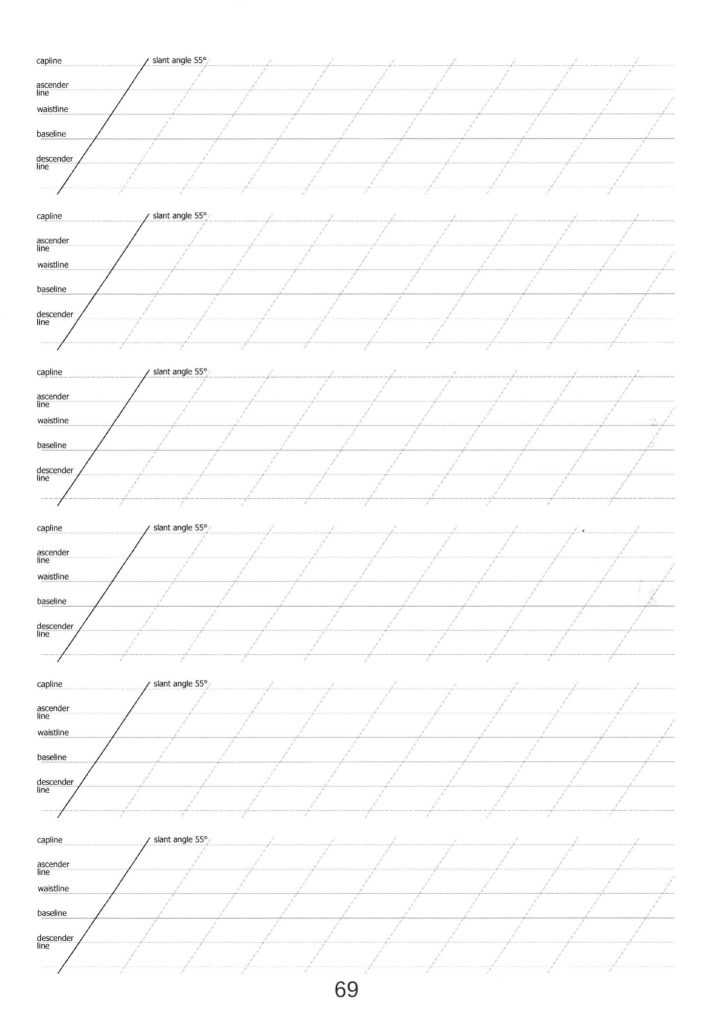

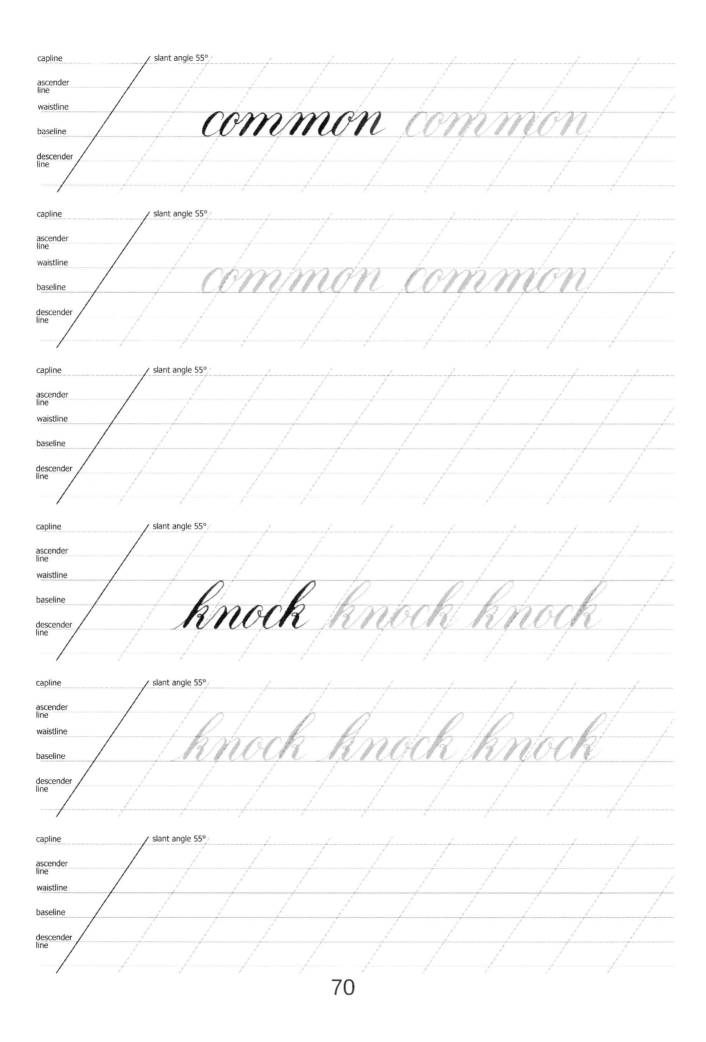

capline
ascender line
waistline
baseline
descender line

slant angle 55°

*common common*

*common common*

*knock knock knock*

*knock knock knock*

70

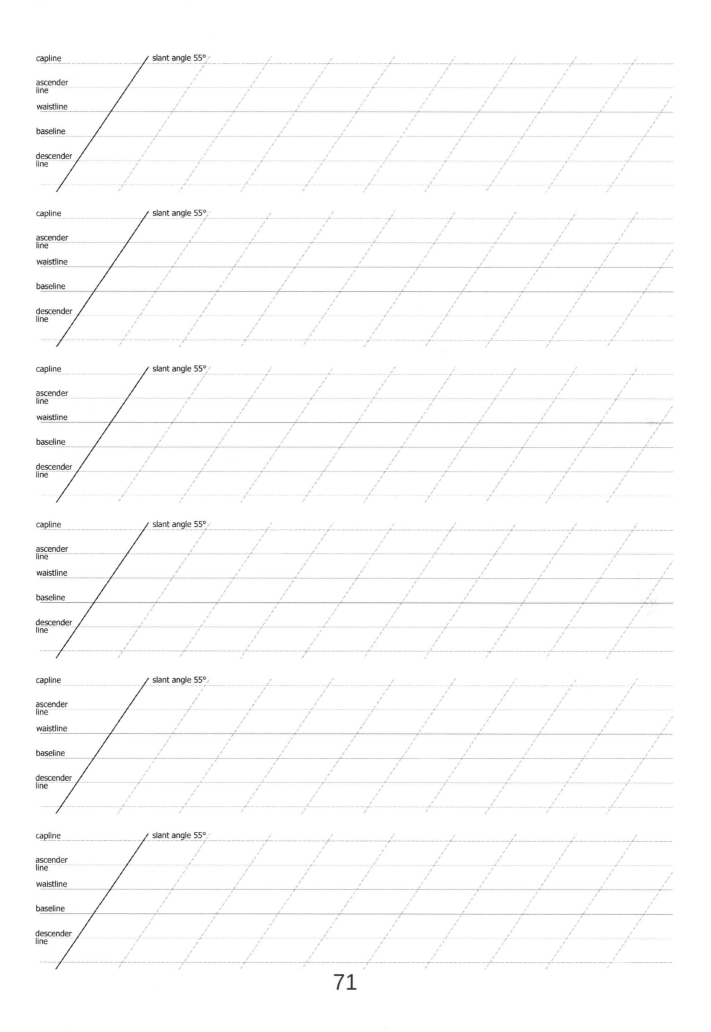

capline
ascender line
waistline
baseline
descender line
slant angle 55°

capline
ascender line
waistline
baseline
descender line
slant angle 55°

capline
ascender line
waistline
baseline
descender line
slant angle 55°

capline
ascender line
waistline
baseline
descender line
slant angle 55°

capline
ascender line
waistline
baseline
descender line
slant angle 55°

capline
ascender line
waistline
baseline
descender line
slant angle 55°

capline
ascender line
waistline
baseline
descender line

slant angle 55°

*little little little little*

capline
ascender line
waistline
baseline
descender line

slant angle 55°

*little little little little*

capline
ascender line
waistline
baseline
descender line

slant angle 55°

capline
ascender line
waistline
baseline
descender line

slant angle 55°

*bubble bubble bubble*

capline
ascender line
waistline
baseline
descender line

slant angle 55°

*bubble bubble bubble*

capline
ascender line
waistline
baseline
descender line

slant angle 55°

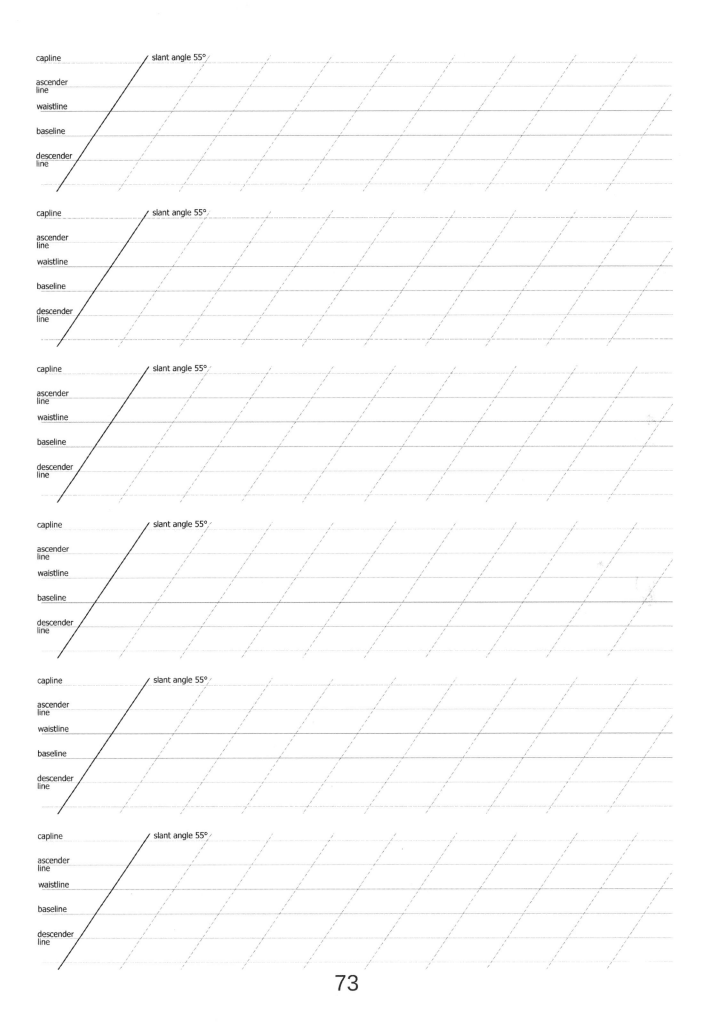

capline

ascender
line

waistline

baseline

descender
line

slant angle 55°

73

capline
ascender line
waistline
baseline
descender line

slant angle 55°

young young young

young young young

quickly quickly quickly

quickly quickly quickly

74

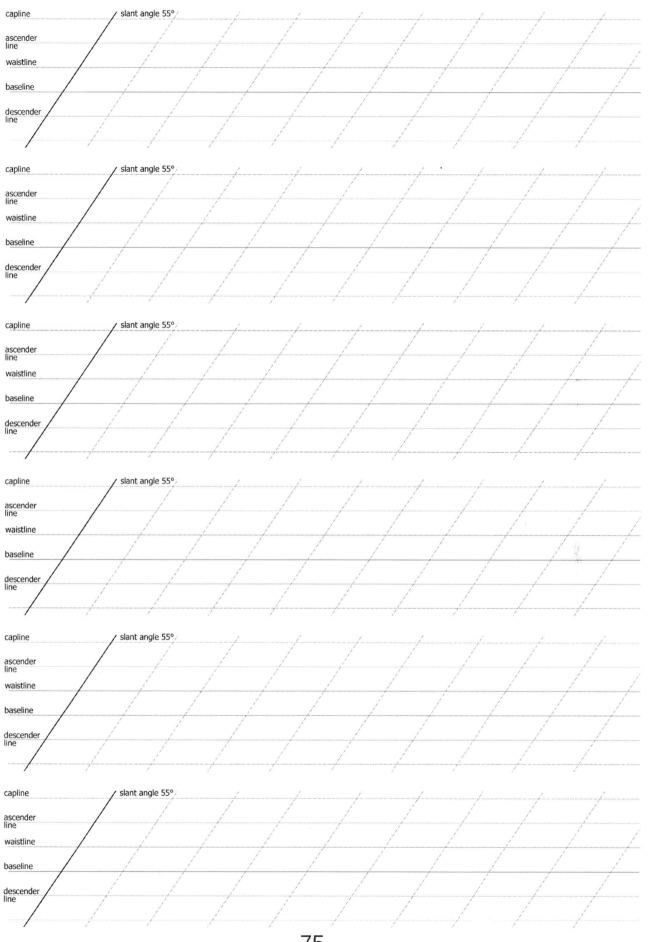

75

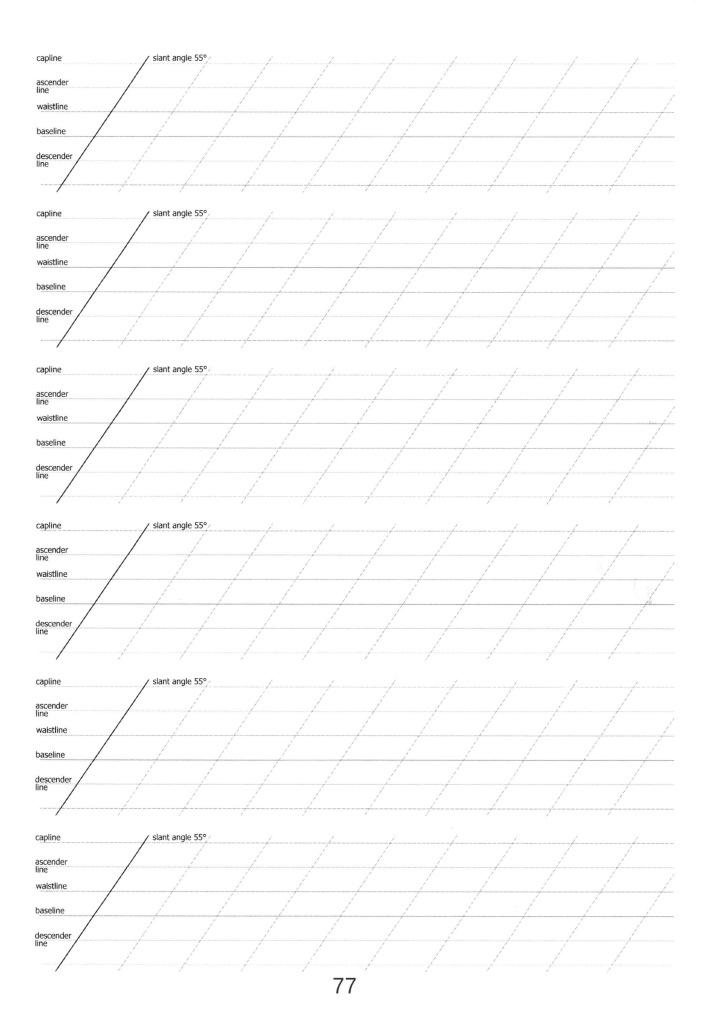

77

# Uppercase Letters

ANML
VW
BPRD
CGEO
QZ
IJ
TF
HK
UY
SX

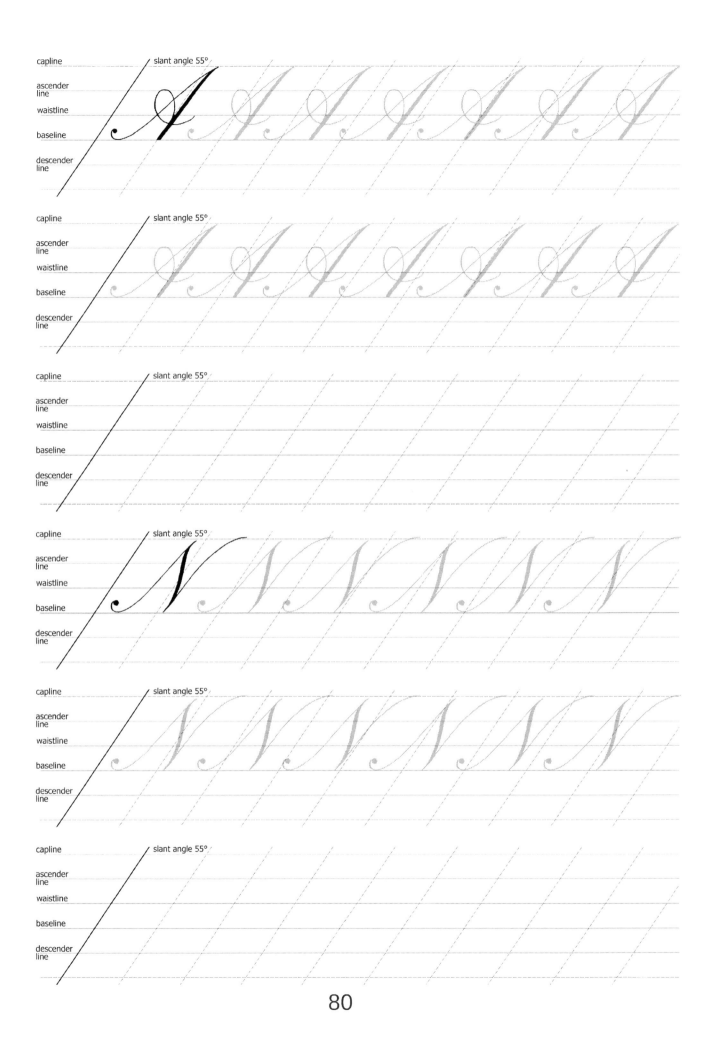

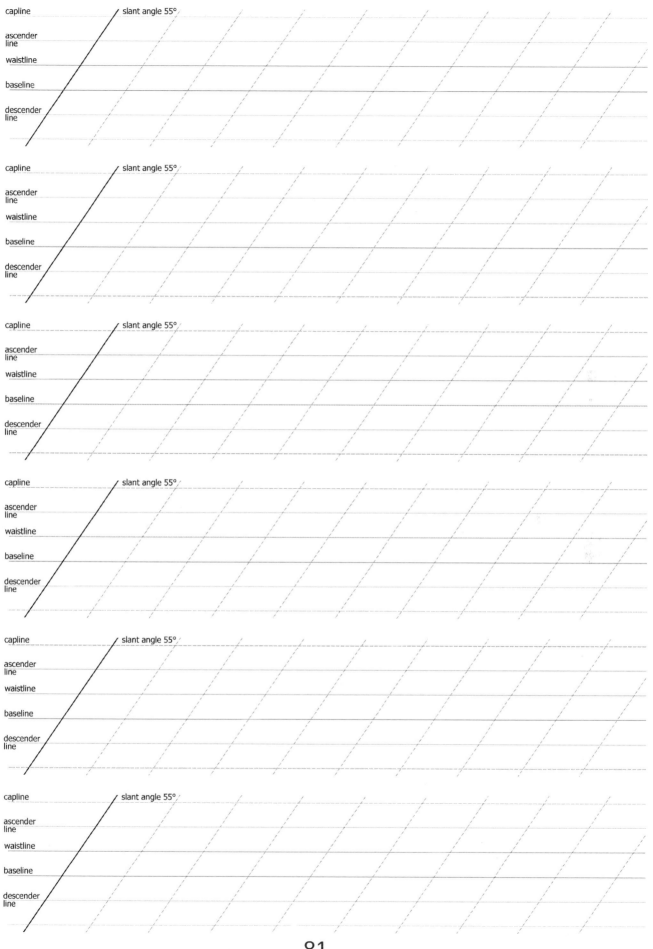

capline
slant angle 55°
ascender line
waistline
baseline
descender line

capline
slant angle 55°
ascender line
waistline
baseline
descender line

capline
slant angle 55°
ascender line
waistline
baseline
descender line

capline
slant angle 55°
ascender line
waistline
baseline
descender line

capline
slant angle 55°
ascender line
waistline
baseline
descender line

capline
slant angle 55°
ascender line
waistline
baseline
descender line

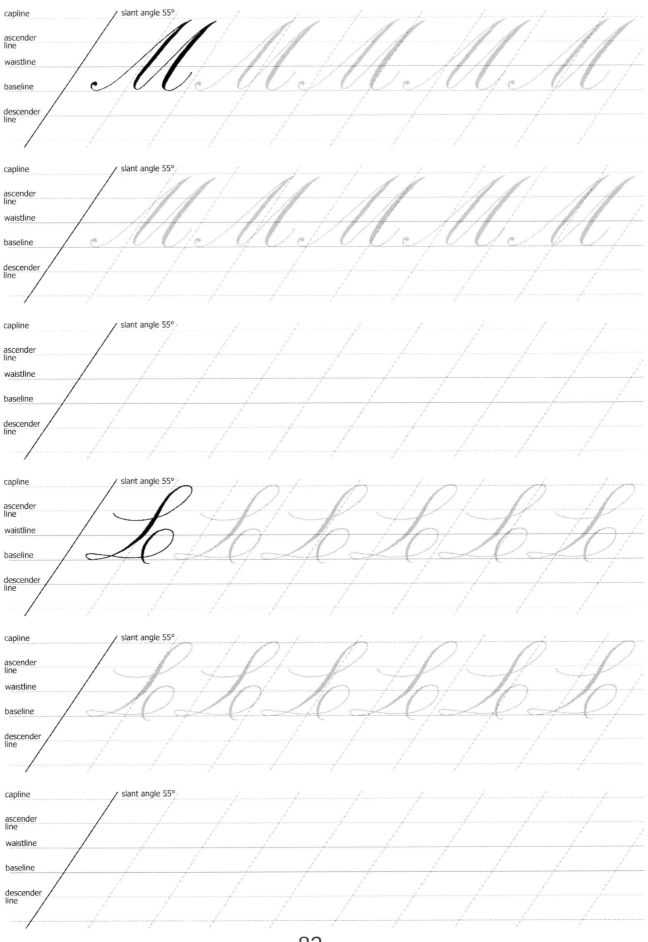

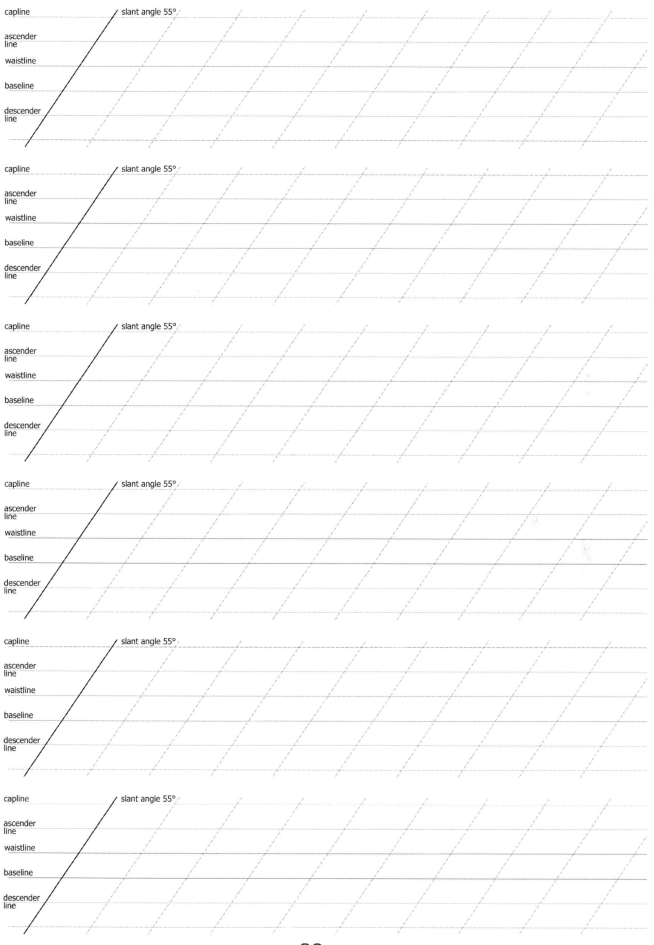

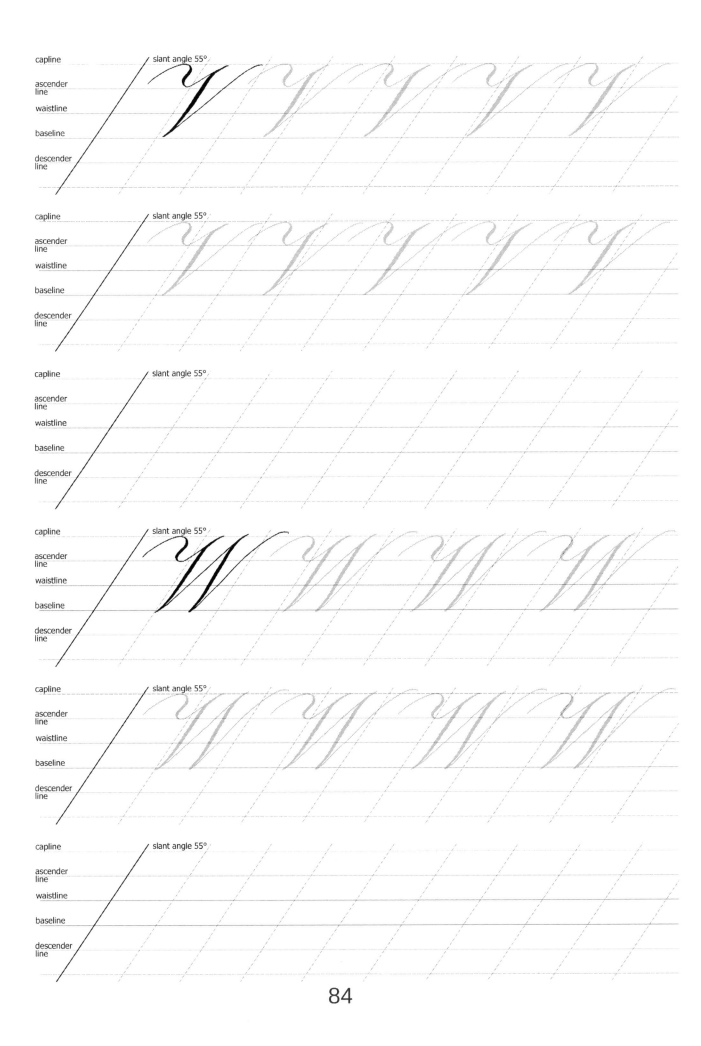

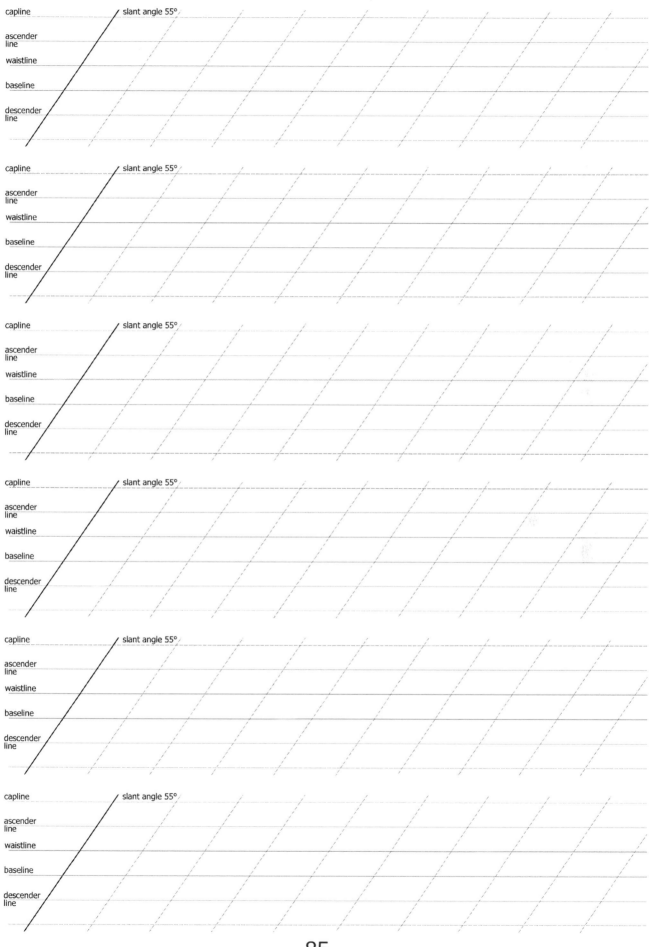

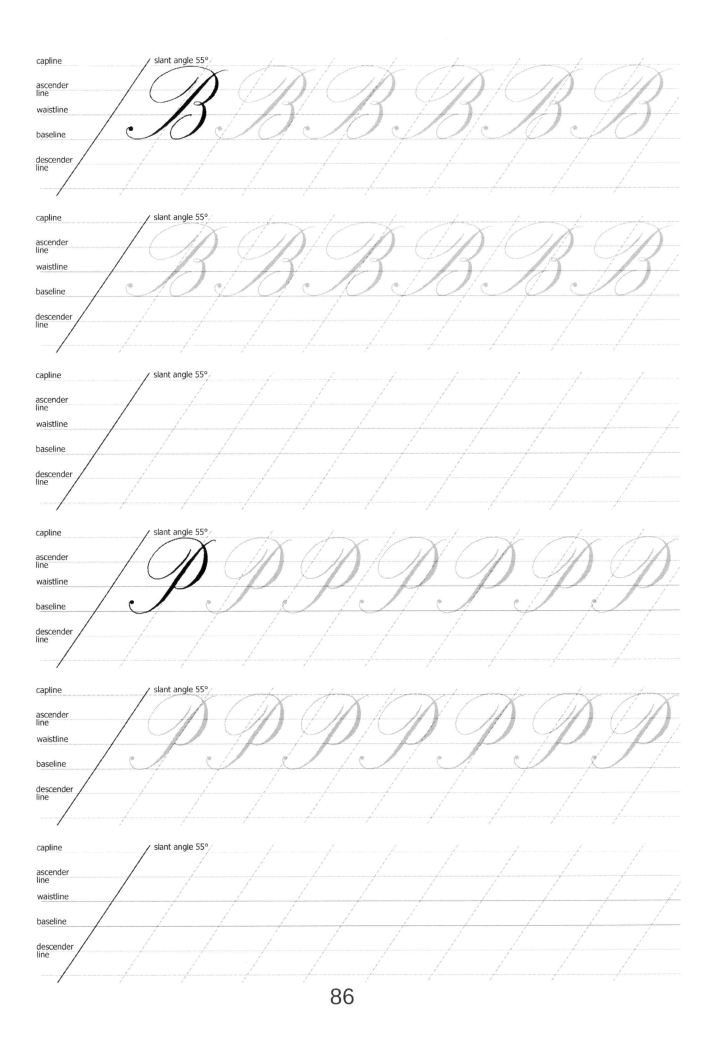

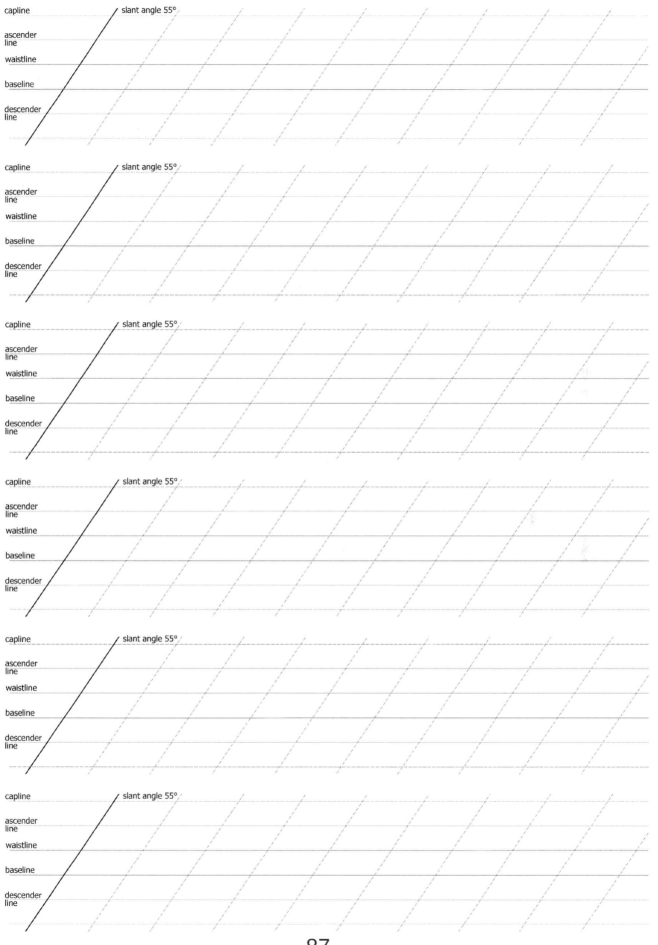

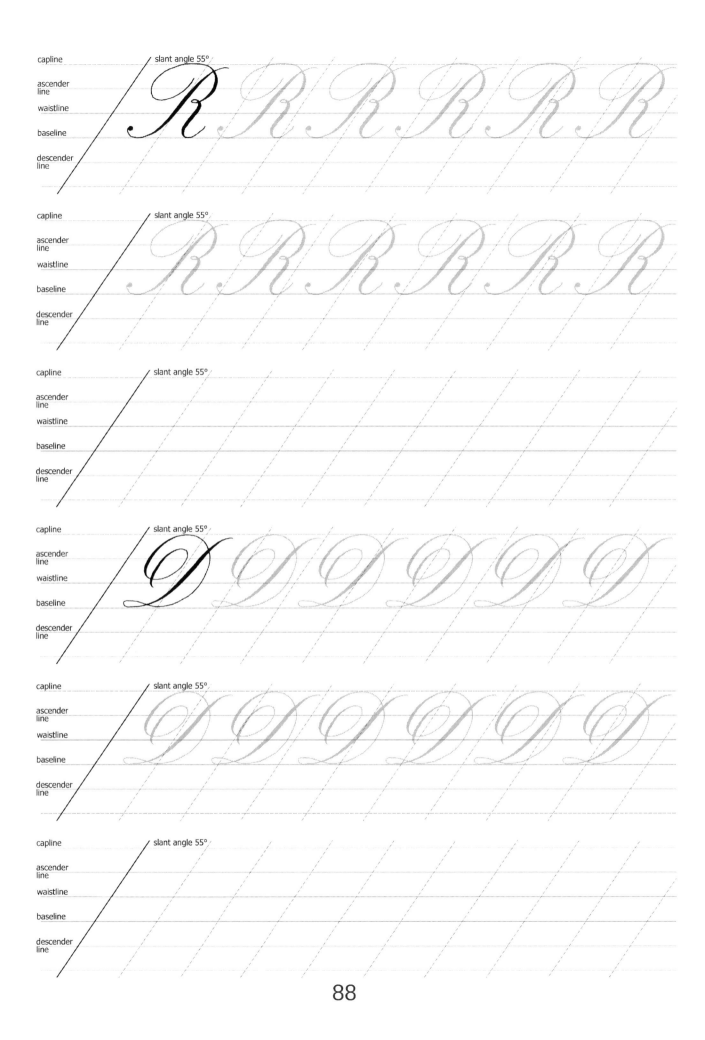

capline
ascender line
waistline
baseline
descender line

slant angle 55°

88

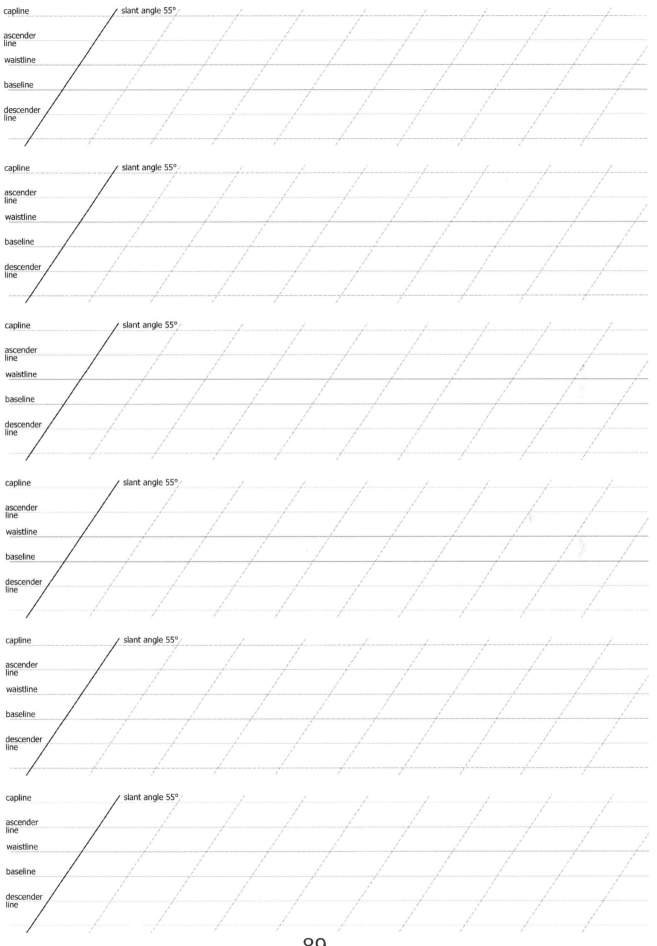

89

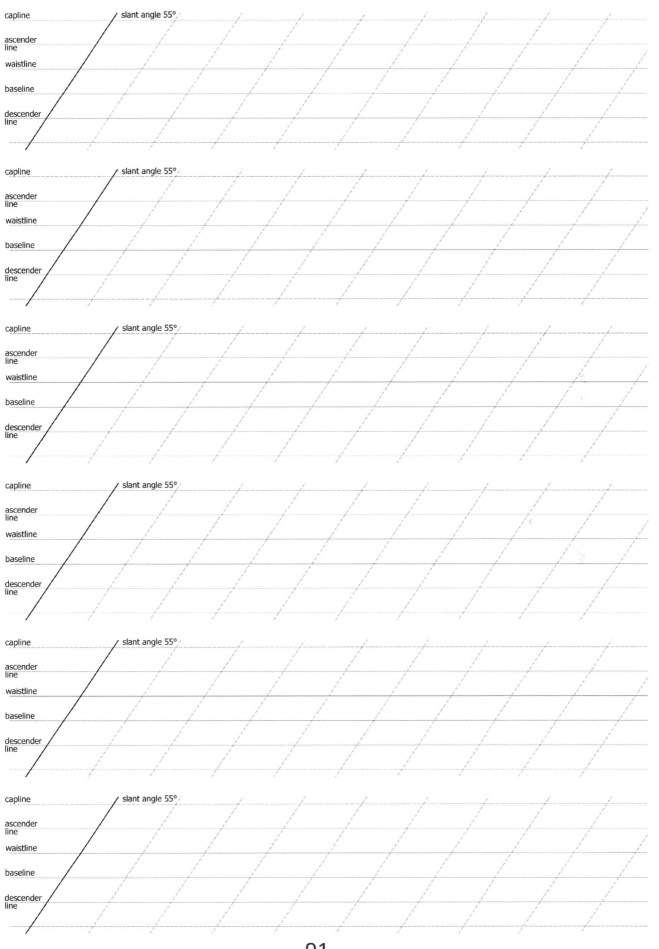

capline

ascender line

waistline

baseline

descender line

slant angle 55°

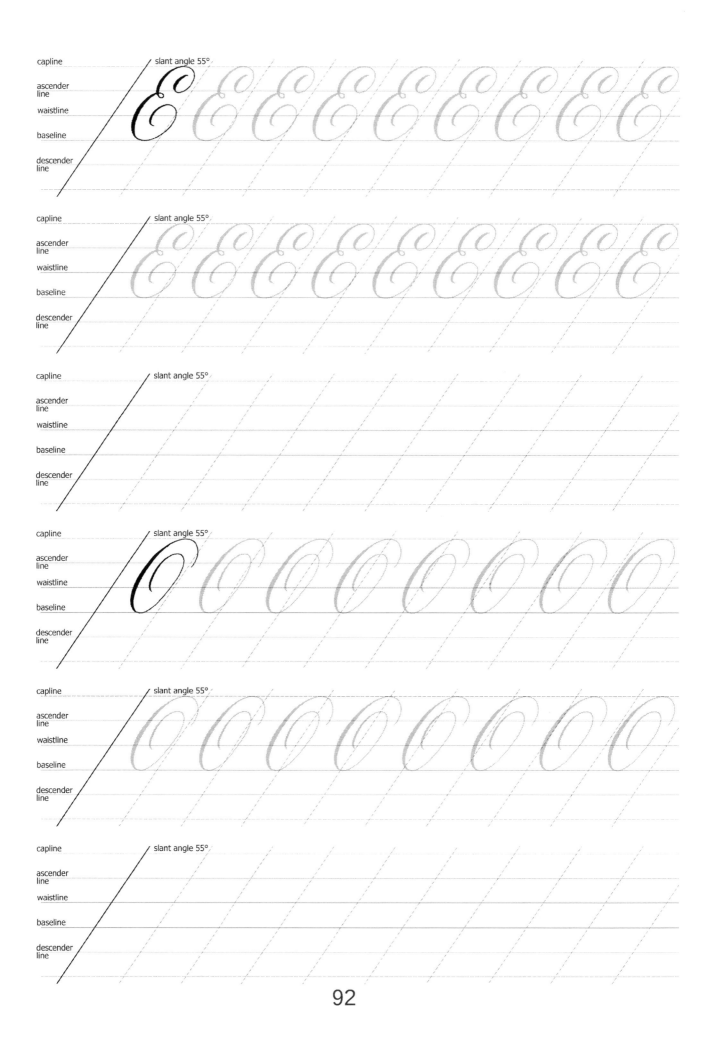

92

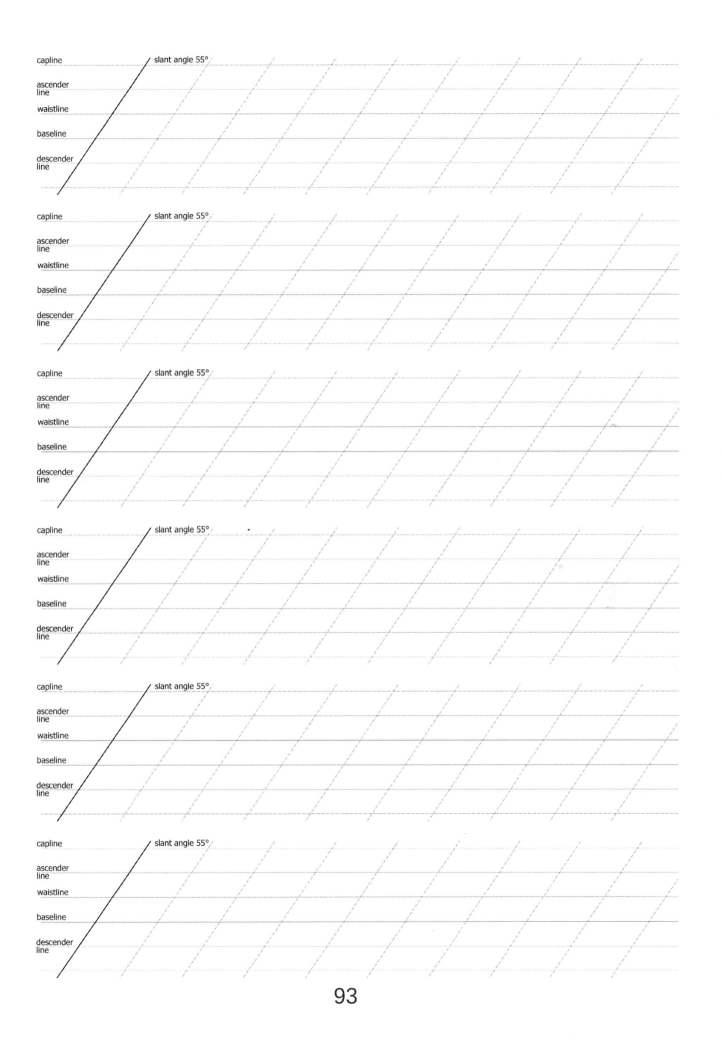

capline
ascender line
waistline
baseline
descender line
slant angle 55°

capline
ascender line
waistline
baseline
descender line
slant angle 55°

capline
ascender line
waistline
baseline
descender line
slant angle 55°

capline
ascender line
waistline
baseline
descender line
slant angle 55°

capline
ascender line
waistline
baseline
descender line
slant angle 55°

capline
ascender line
waistline
baseline
descender line
slant angle 55°

93

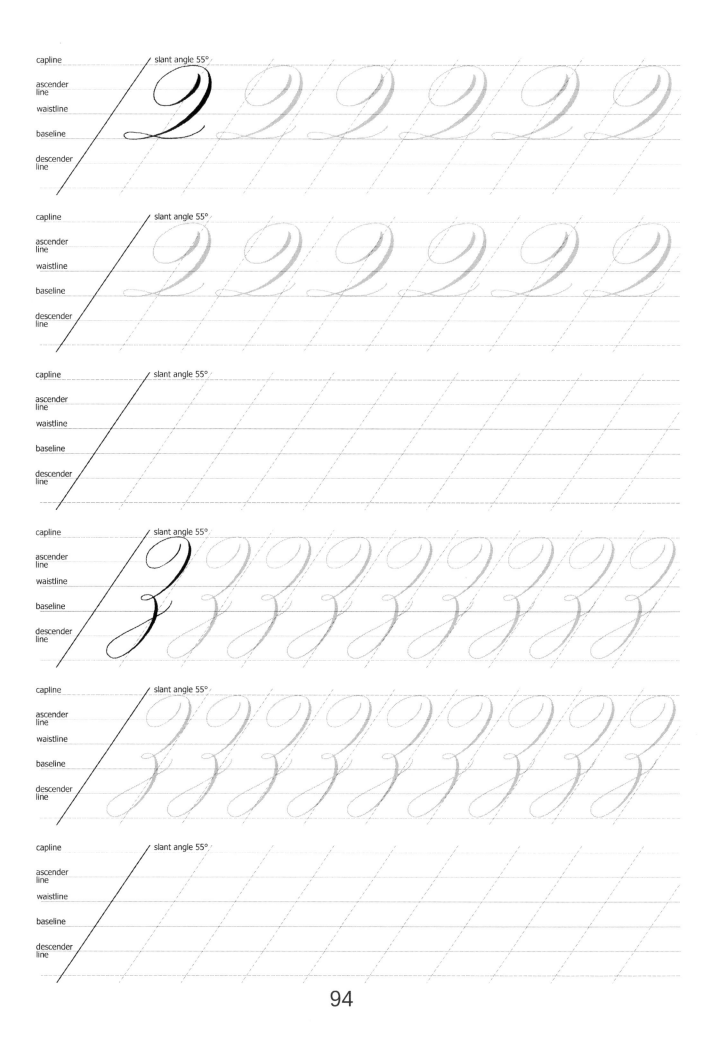

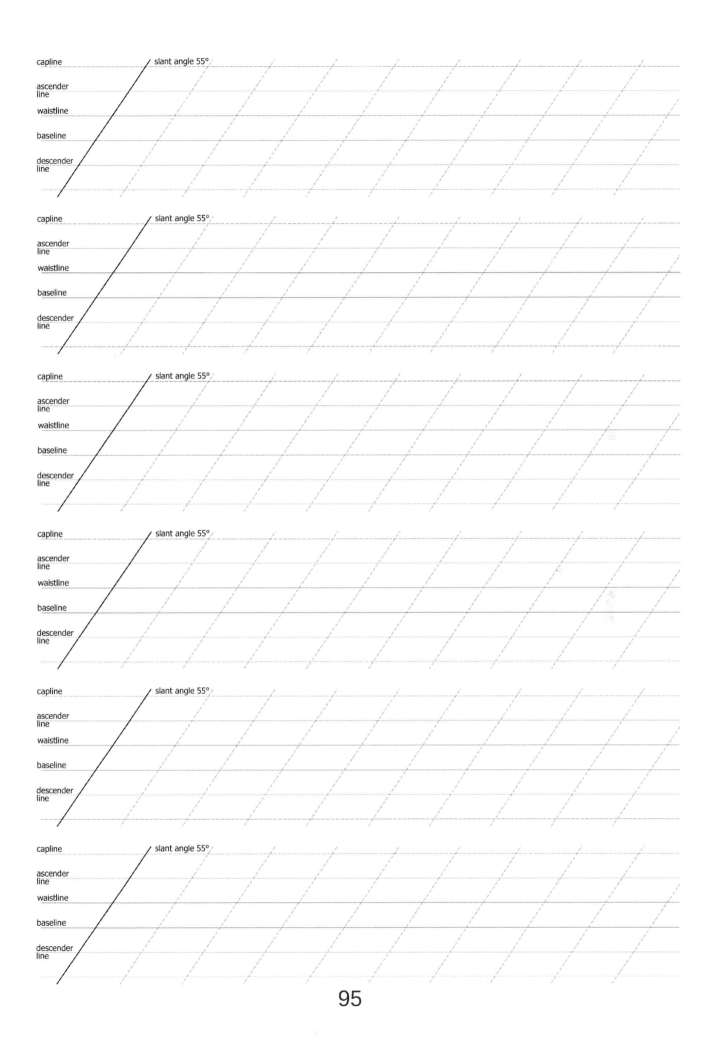

95

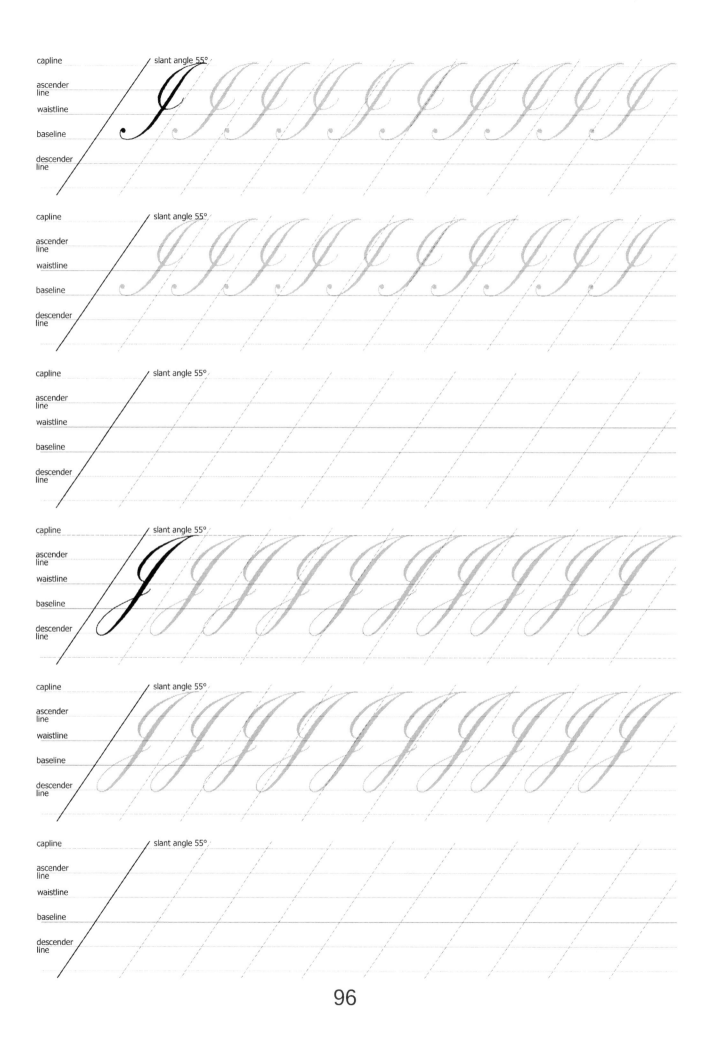

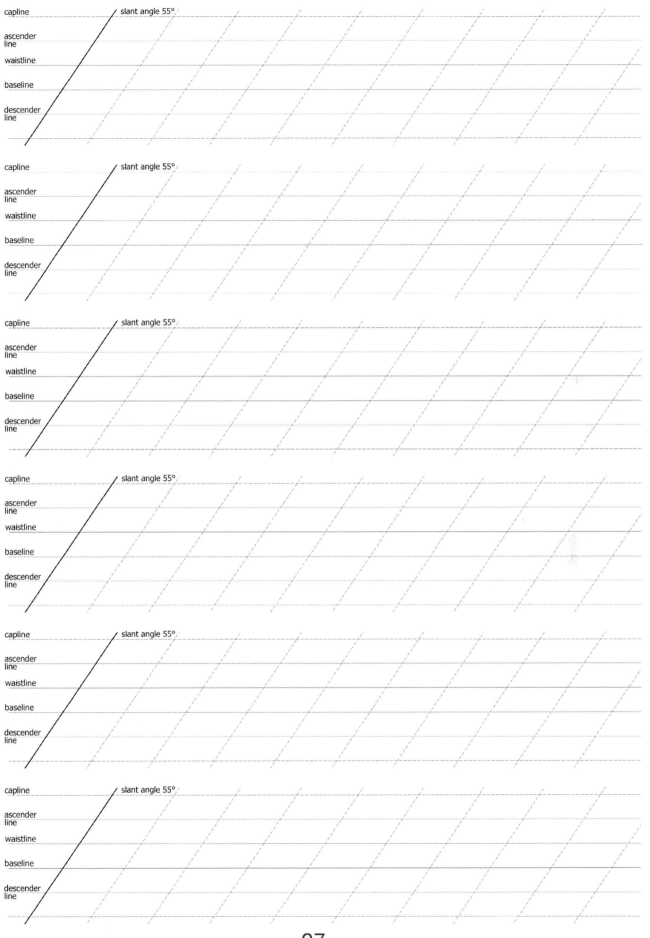

capline

ascender line

waistline

baseline

descender line

slant angle 55°

capline

ascender line

waistline

baseline

descender line

slant angle 55°

capline

ascender line

waistline

baseline

descender line

slant angle 55°

capline

ascender line

waistline

baseline

descender line

slant angle 55°

capline

ascender line

waistline

baseline

descender line

slant angle 55°

capline

ascender line

waistline

baseline

descender line

slant angle 55°

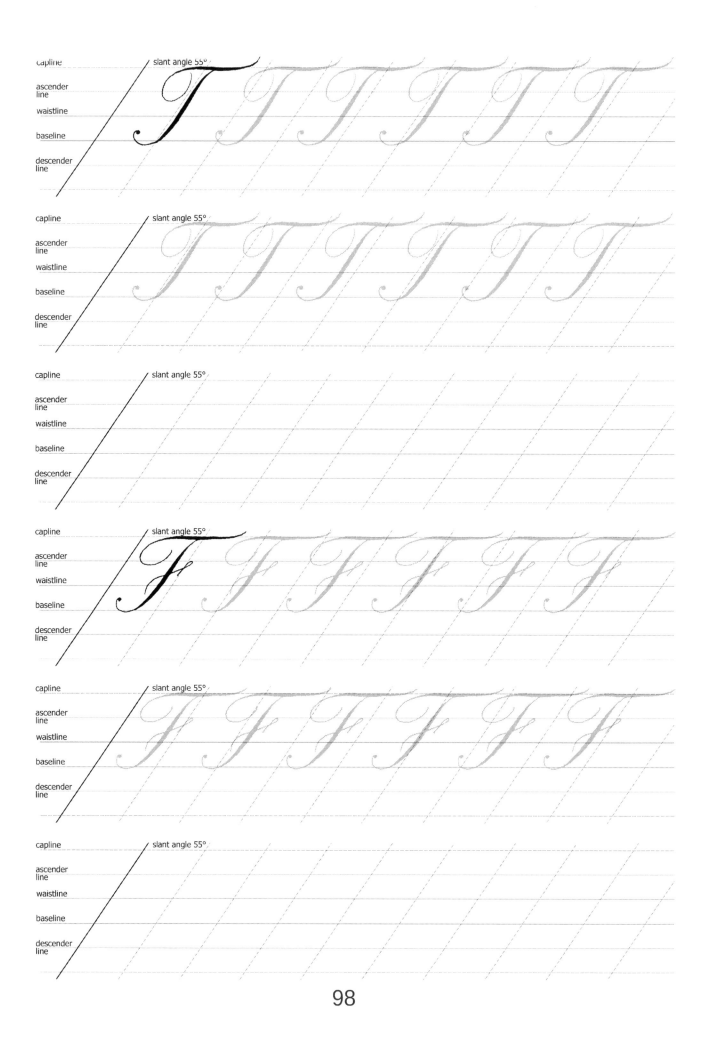

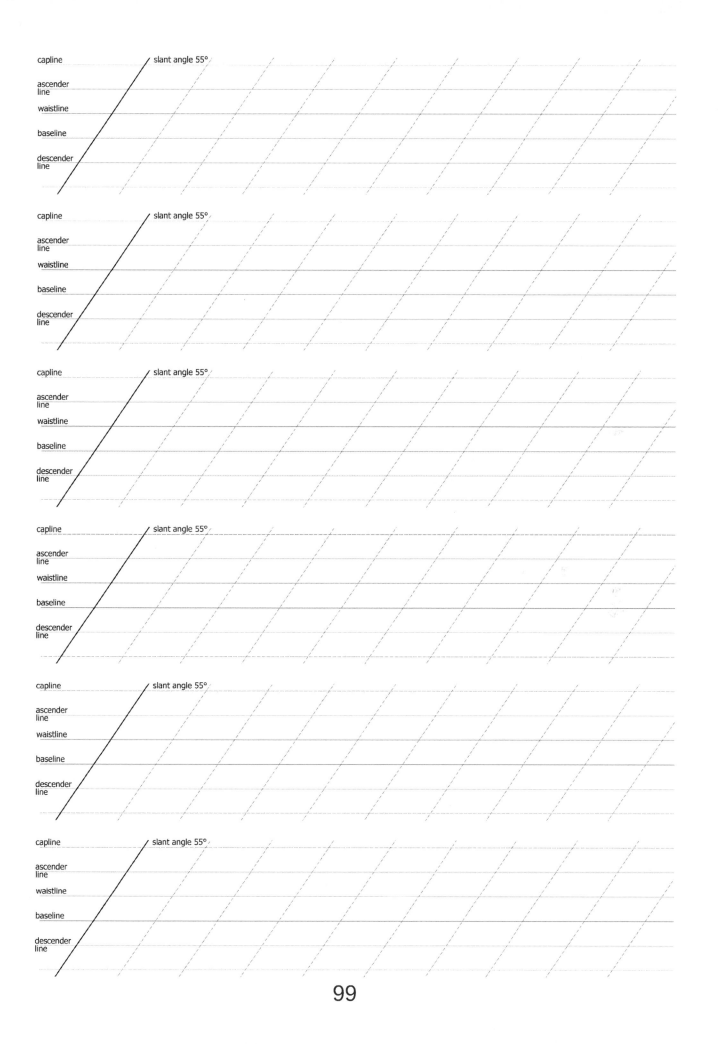

capline

ascender
line

waistline

baseline

descender
line

slant angle 55°

capline

ascender
line

waistline

baseline

descender
line

slant angle 55°

capline

ascender
line

waistline

baseline

descender
line

slant angle 55°

capline

ascender
line

waistline

baseline

descender
line

slant angle 55°

capline

ascender
line

waistline

baseline

descender
line

slant angle 55°

capline

ascender
line

waistline

baseline

descender
line

slant angle 55°

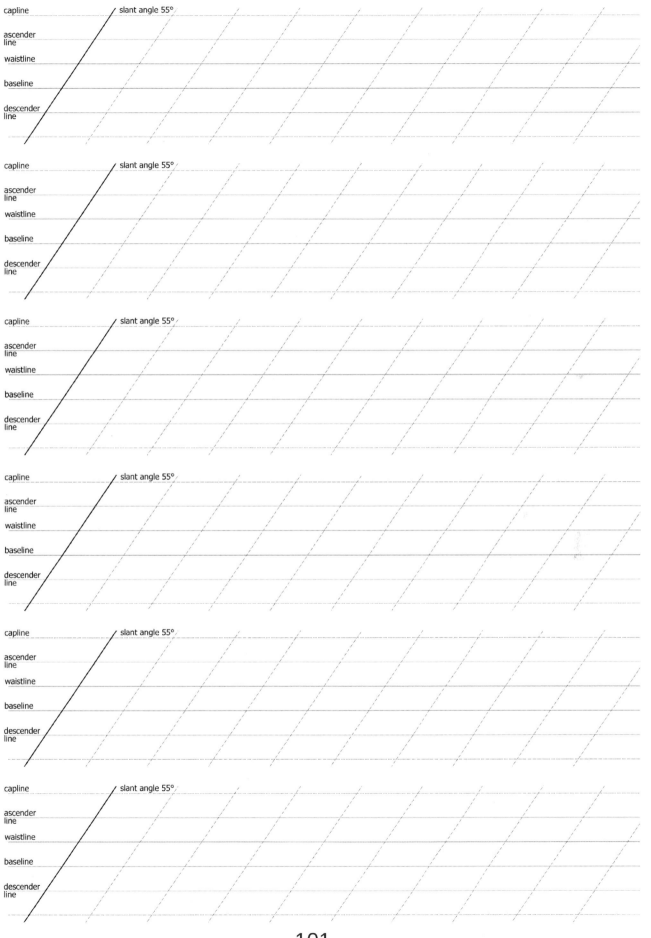

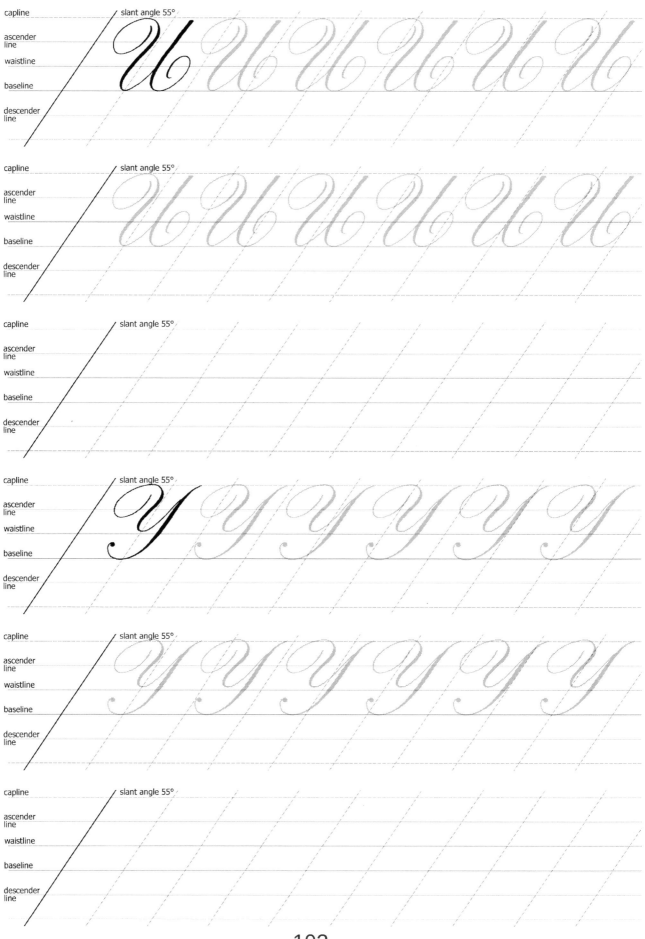

capline
ascender line
waistline
baseline
descender line

slant angle 55°

102

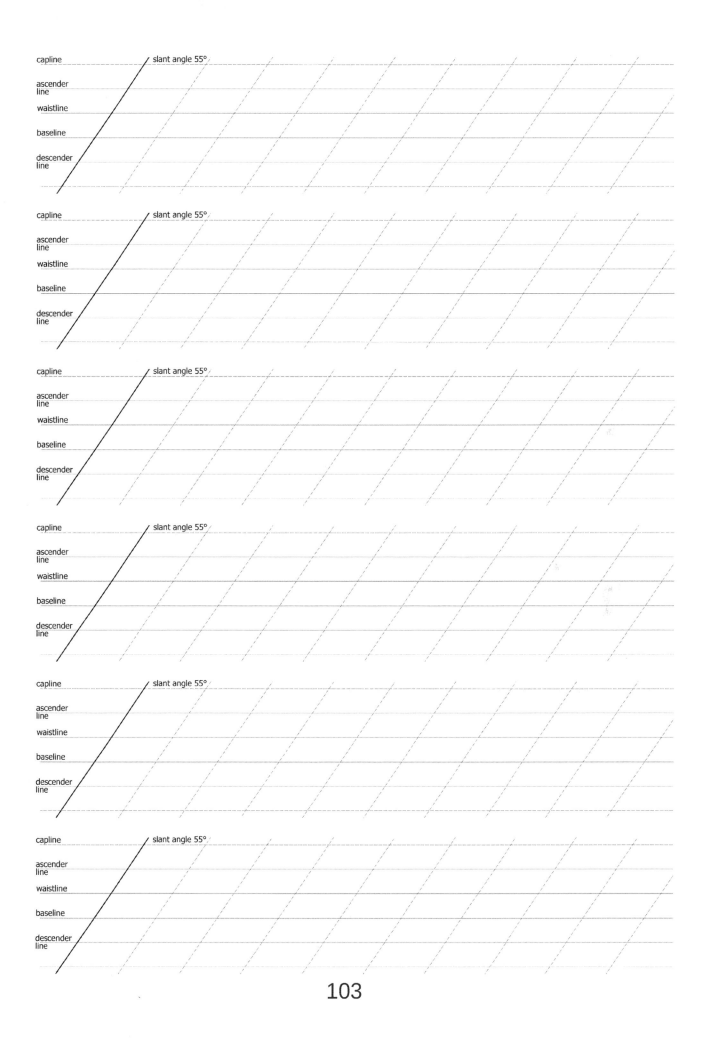

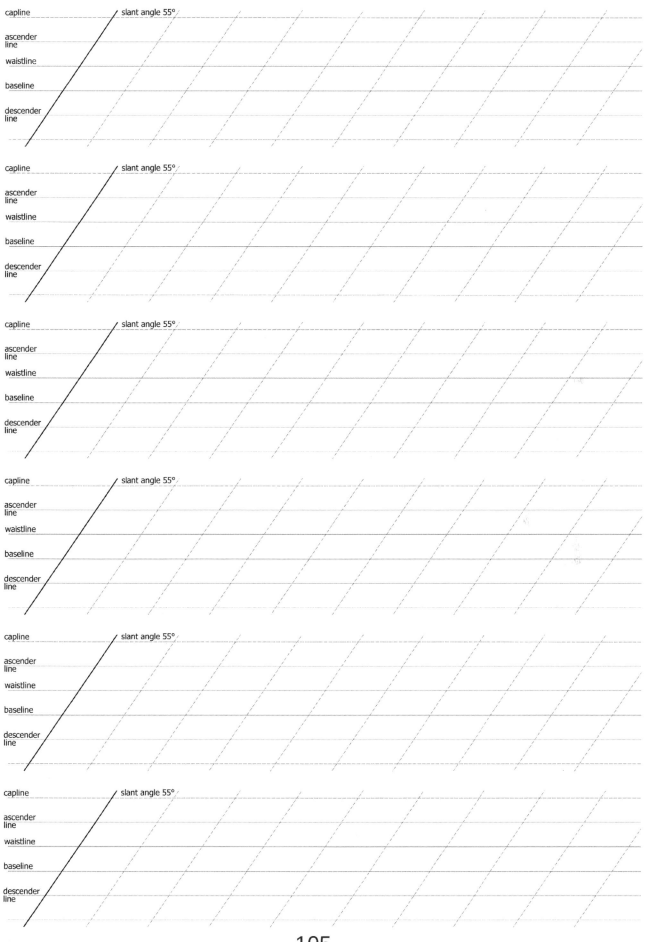

# Writing Sentences

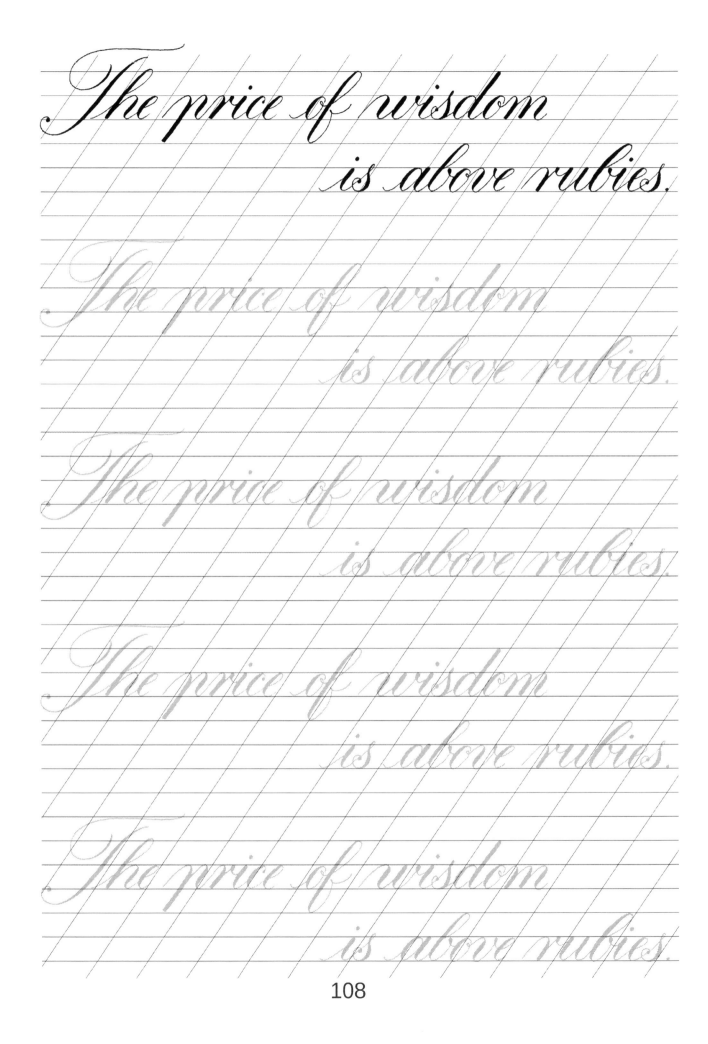

The price of wisdom
is above rubies.

109

The child is
the father of the man.

111

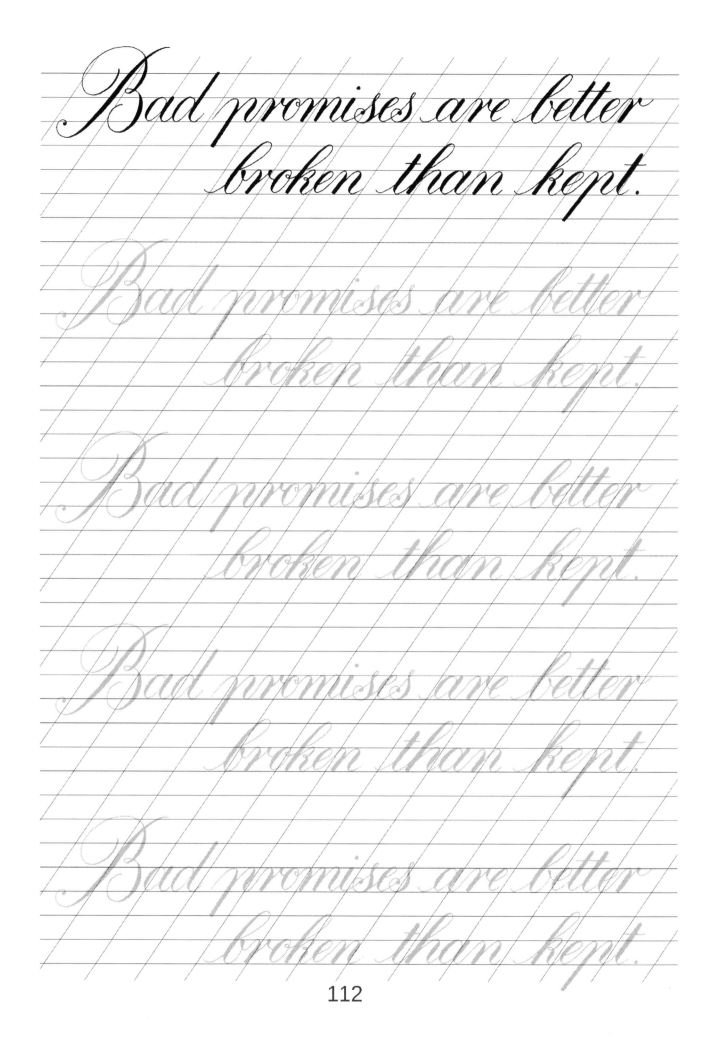

Bad promises are better
broken than kept.

113

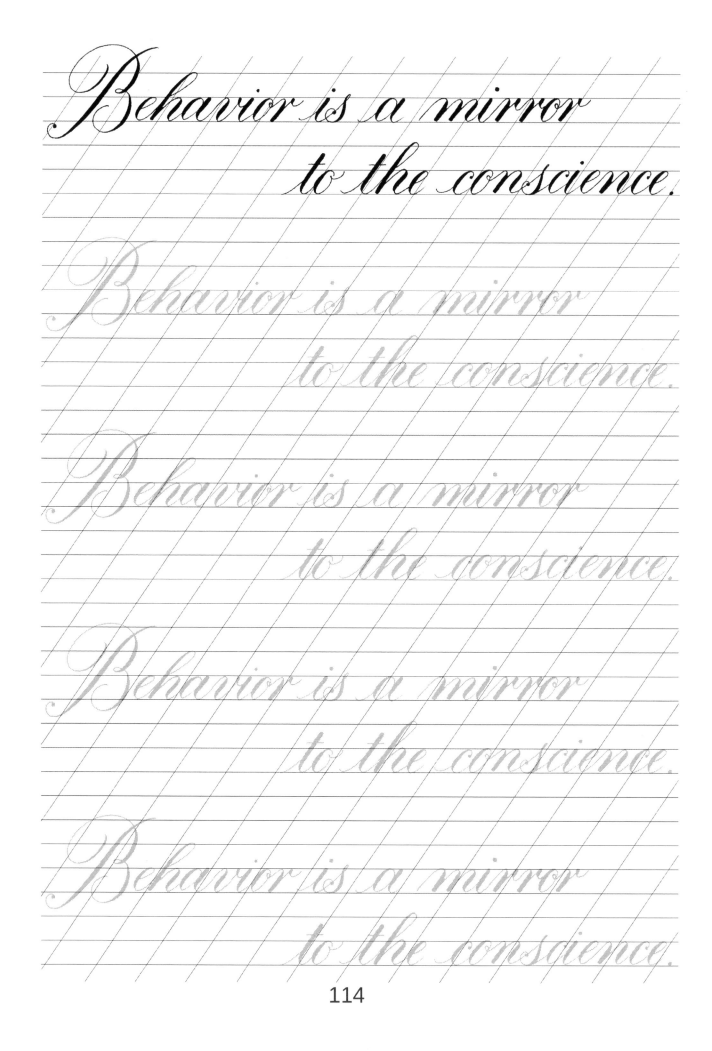

Behavior is a mirror
to the conscience.

115

There is no poverty comparable to the want of patience.

There is no poverty comparable to the want of patience.

There is no poverty comparable to the want of patience.

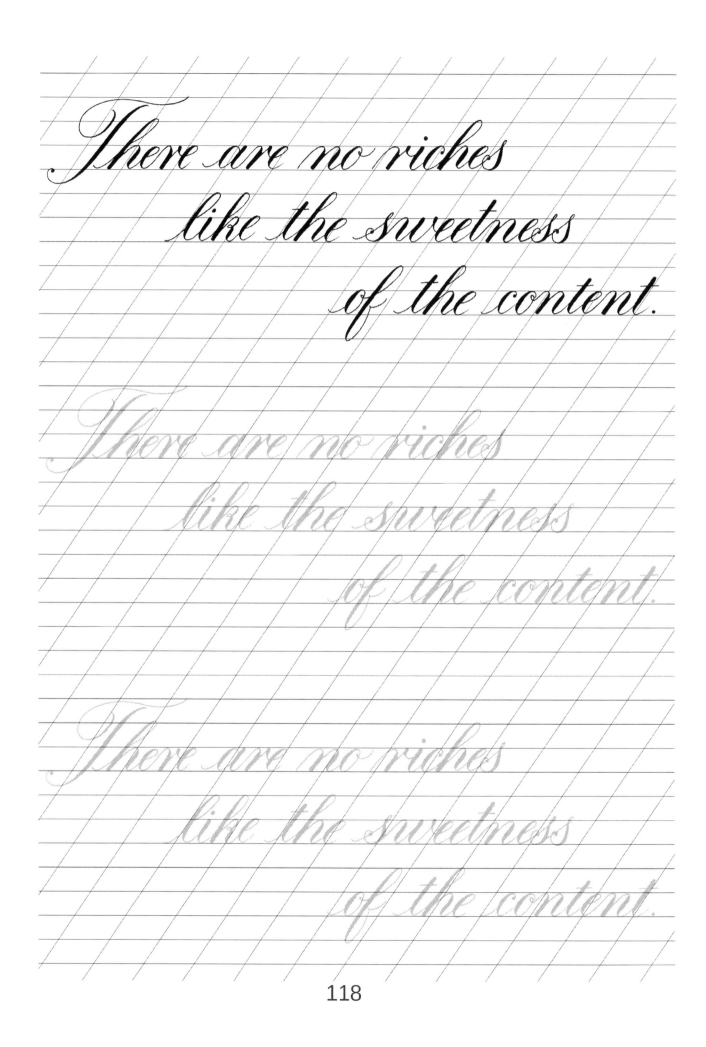

There are no riches
like the sweetness
of the content.

119

Grace was
in all her steps;
heaven in her eyes.

Grace was
in all her steps;
heaven in her eyes.

Grace was
in all her steps;
heaven in her eyes.

121

It is only when it is bent
that the bow shows
its strength.

It is only when it is bent
that the bow shows
its strength.

122

123

Every shadow points
to the sun.

Every shadow points
to the sun.

125

Mercy's gate opens
to those who knock.

Mercy's gate opens
to those who knock.

O what a tangled
web we weave
When first we practice
to deceive.

O what a tangled
web we weave
When first we practice
to deceive.

129

Secrets make a dungeon of the heart and a jailer of its owner.

131

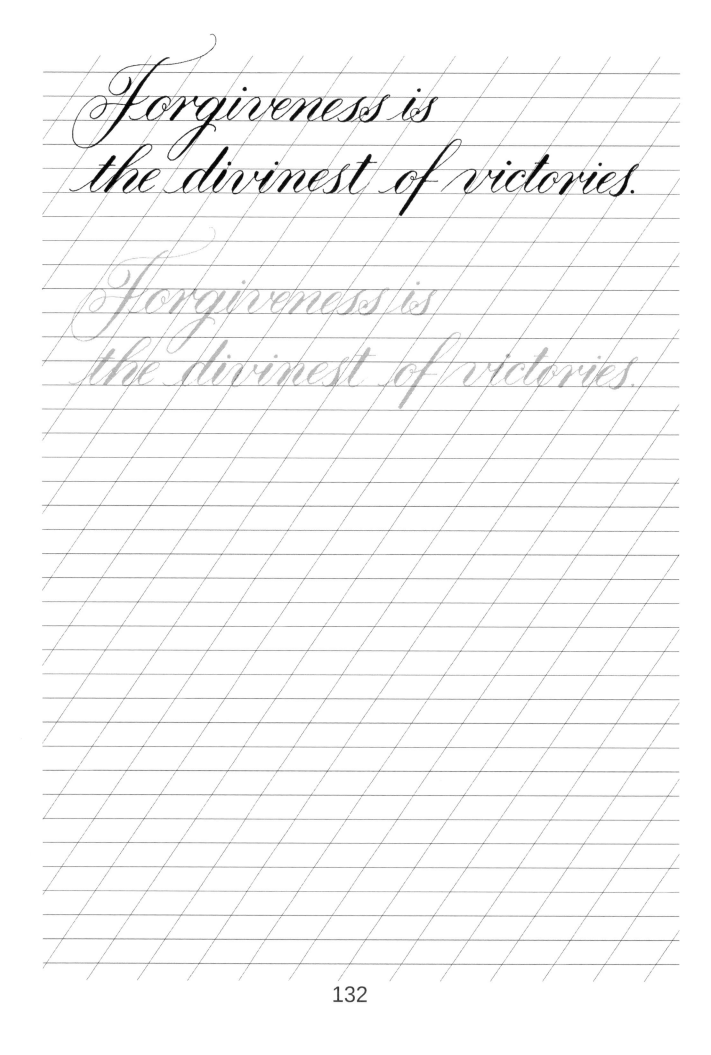

Forgiveness is
the divinest of victories.

Forgiveness is
the divinest of victories.

132

133

Made in United States
Troutdale, OR
03/23/2024

18681442R00077